Create, Then Take a Break: 250 Anecdotes and Stories

David Bruce

Published by David Bruce, 2022.

CREATE, THEN TAKE A BREAK: 250 ANECDOTES AND STORIES

First edition. October 8, 2022.

Copyright © 2022 David Bruce.

ISBN: 979-8215440872

Written by David Bruce.

Table of Contents

Dedication

Dedicated to Carl Eugene Bruce and Josephine Saturday Bruce

My father, Carl Eugene Bruce, died on 24 October 2013. He used to work for Ohio Power, and at one time, his job was to shut off the electricity of people who had not paid their bills. He sometimes would find a home with an impoverished mother and some children. Instead of shutting off their electricity, he would tell the mother that she needed to pay her bill or soon her electricity would be shut off. He would write on a form that no one was home when he stopped by because if no one was home he did not have to shut off their electricity.

The best good deed that anyone ever did for my father occurred after a storm that knocked down many power lines. He and other linemen worked long hours and got wet and cold. Their feet were freezing because water got into their boots and soaked their socks. Fortunately, a kind woman gave my father and the other linemen dry socks to wear.

My mother, Josephine Saturday Bruce, died on 14 June 2003. She used to work at a store that sold clothing. One day, an impoverished mother with a baby clothed in rags walked into the store and started shoplifting in an interesting way: The mother took the rags off her baby and dressed the infant in new clothing. My mother knew that this mother could not afford to buy the clothing, but she helped the mother dress her baby and then she watched as the mother walked out of the store without paying.

***

The doing of good deeds is important. As a free person, you can choose to live your life as a good person or as a bad person. To be a good person, do good deeds. To be a bad person, do bad deeds. If you do good deeds, you will become good. If you do bad deeds, you will become bad. To become the person you want to be, act as if you already are that kind of person. Each of us chooses what kind of person we will become. To become a good person, do the things a good person does. To become a bad person, do the things a bad person does. The opportunity to take action to become the kind of person you want to be is yours.

Human beings have free will. According to the Babylonian Niddah 16b, whenever a baby is to be conceived, the Lailah (angel in charge of contraception) takes the drop of semen that will result in the conception and asks God, "Sovereign of the Universe, what is going to be the fate of this drop? Will it develop into a robust or into a weak person? An intelligent or a stupid person? A wealthy or a poor person?" The Lailah asks all these questions, but it does not ask, "Will it develop into a righteous or a wicked person?" The answer to that question lies in the decisions to be freely made by the human being that is the result of the conception.

A Buddhist monk visiting a class wrote this on the chalkboard: "EVERYONE WANTS TO SAVE THE WORLD, BUT NO ONE WANTS TO HELP MOM DO THE DISHES." The students laughed, but the monk then said, "Statistically, it's highly unlikely that any of you will ever have the opportunity to run into a burning orphanage and rescue an infant. But, in the smallest gesture of kindness — a warm smile, holding the door for the person behind you, shoveling the driveway of the elderly person next door — you have committed an act of immeasurable profundity, because to each of us, our life is our universe."

In her book titled *I Have Chosen to Stay and Fight*, comedian Margaret Cho writes, "I believe that we get complimentary snack-size portions of the afterlife, and we all receive them in a different way." For Ms. Cho, many of her snack-size portions of the afterlife come in hip hop music. Other people get different snack-size portions of the afterlife, and we all must be on the lookout for them when they come our way. And perhaps doing good deeds and experiencing good deeds are snack-size portions of the afterlife.

The Zen master Gisan was taking a bath. The water was too hot, so he asked a student to add some cold water to the bath. The student brought a bucket of cold water, added some cold water to the bath, and then threw the rest of the water on a rocky path. Gisan scolded the student: "Everything can be used. Why did you waste the rest of the water by pouring it on the path? There are some plants nearby which could have used the water. What right do you have to waste even a drop of water?" The student became enlightened and changed his name to Tekisui, which means "Drop of Water."

Cover Photograph for *Create, Then Take a Break: 250 Anecdotes and Stories*:

https://pixabay.com/photos/woman-relaxation-beach-leisure-6714008/

***

This is a short, quick, and easy read.

Anecdotes are usually short humorous stories. Sometimes they are thought-provoking or informative, not amusing.

***

Educate Yourself
Read Like A Wolf Eats
Be Excellent to Each Other
Books Then, Books Now, Books Forever

***

Do you know a language other than English? If you do, I give you permission to translate this book, copyright your translation, publish or self-publish it, and keep all the royalties for yourself. (Do give me credit, of course, for the original book.)

Chapter 1: From Actors and Acting to Comedians and Humorists

Actors and Acting

• English actor Stanley Holloway, who created the role of Eliza Doolittle's father in *My Fair Lady* on Broadway, almost didn't. He felt ignored during rehearsals, although he later realized that that was a compliment. The director and everyone else were concentrating on Rex Harrison, who was unknown—at that time—as a musical comedy star. Knowing that Mr. Holloway was an extremely competent actor, they left him to his own devices. Mr. Holloway called the play's producer, Herman Levin, and asked to be released from his contract because no one was even saying hello when he arrived at the theater. Mr. Levin talked him out of immediately quitting and the next morning when Mr. Holloway arrived at the theater, everyone crowded around him to say hello. Even though Mr. Holloway knew that it was a put-up job, he felt better.[1]

• When Marilyn Monroe showed up to act the part of an aging jewel thief's girlfriend in *The Asphalt Jungle*, she told the director, John Huston, how nervous she was. He replied, "If you're not nervous, you might as well give up!" By the way, Ms. Monroe was known for being late everywhere. She once stopped to apply more lipstick—and missed her plane. Also by the way, one of the most famous scenes in Ms. Monroe's movies occurs in *The Seven Year Itch*, where she stands on a grating above a subway on a hot night and the subway train causes a cooling breeze that makes her skirt fly into the air. This scene was filmed at 2 in the morning; nevertheless, over 2,000 people were on hand to watch it.[2]

• John Barrymore was noted as much for his dissipation as for his acting. While acting in *Hamlet* after a night of revelry, he began the "To be or not to be" soliloquy, but in the middle of the speech found it necessary to retire to the side of the stage so he could vomit. Later, he was complimented for this innovation: "I say, Barrymore, that was the most daring and perhaps the most effective innovation ever offered. I refer to your deliberate pausing in the midst of the soliloquy to retire, almost, from the scene. May I congratulate you upon such imaginative business? You seemed quite distraught. But it was effective!"[3]

• The famous actor Edmund Kean idolized fellow actor George Frederick Cooke. He even had a monument erected over Mr. Cooke's grave in New York and carried away one of Mr. Cooke's finger bones, which he displayed on a mantle. Mr. Kean's wife, however, objected to the display of the finger bone, and so one day it became "lost." Like many other actors, Mr. Kean studied life to gain effects to use in acting. Once, he was wounded while fencing, and he fainted. When he regained consciousness, his first words were, "How did I fall?"[4]

• As a young actor, John Gielgud discussed his plans with Lilian Baylis, founder of the Old Vic. Anxious to impress, Mr. Gielgud, who had had a successful season at the Old Vic, told Ms. Baylis that he wanted to work there again but that he had many other engagements. Ms. Baylis put the young actor in his place by telling him, "That's right, dear. You play all the young parts you can—while you're still able to."[5]

• Actor Gene Barry, who was named Eugene Klass at birth, played Bat Masterson on television from 1959 to 1961. Once he stopped to buy a *tallith* (a fringed prayer shawl) for his son's bar mitzvah. The man who waited on him at the store looked at his check, then asked, "Are you Gene Barry?" He replied that he was, and the man ran to the back of the store and yelled to his wife, "BAT MASTERSON IS JEWISH."[6]

• Natalie Schafer, who played Mrs. Thurston Howell on *Gilligan's Island*, always kept her age a secret. Whenever she went to the doctor's and the doctor asked her for her age, she always told the doctor to look up what age she had said during her last appointment. However, checking on her last appointment never revealed her age, because she been using that trick all her adult life.[7]

• When she was an old lady, former heartthrob Sarah Bernhardt had an apartment at the top of an apartment building. A former suitor visited her and, huffing and puffing after climbing so many stairs, asked her why she had her apartment so high up. Ms. Bernhardt replied, "Nowadays, it's the only way I am still able to make men's hearts beat a little faster."[8]

• Sir Peregrine Plinge once gave a bad performance as Macbeth, so he told a fellow actor, "Give me £5." When the actor asked why, Sir Peregrine threatened, "Because if you don't, I shall tell everybody that you played Macduff to my Macbeth." (Sir Peregrine even went to the box office and said that the play was so bad he wanted his money back.)[9]

• Actress East Robertson once said in a play, "Oh, God, where will I be when my beauty fades!" A voice from the audience said, "In the gutter, love." Ms. Robertson was well known for playing bitchy characters, and during another performance on stage, another voice came from the audience, saying, "I bet you are a bitch off as well as on!"[10]

• Bob Denver is widely known as Gilligan of *Gilligan's Island*, the TV series about a group of people who set out for a three-hour tour, were shipwrecked, and spent three years on an island. Every time Mr. Denver rents a boat, he knows he's going to hear the same joke: "Three-hour tour, huh? We'll never see this boat again, will we?"[11]

Alcohol

• New Zealanders apparently don't drink martinis—or at least they didn't. When comic singer Anna Russell was performing in New Zealand, she threw a party, giving instructions to a bartender to make martinis using Fleischmann's gin. Halfway through the party, however, the martinis began to be dark brown instead of clear. She investigated and discovered that the bartender had run out of Fleischmann's gin, so he was using Fleischmann's whiskey instead. (The party was a success nevertheless.) By the way, in San Francisco, Ms. Russell was invited to a party in a restaurant. The liquor was still flowing at 3 p.m., although a law prohibited liquor at that time. When Ms. Russell worried that the restaurant might get busted, the man sitting next to her said there was no chance of that happening. She asked, "Why?" He replied, "Because I'm the sheriff."[12]

• A bottle of beer can come in handy. When the Globe Theater, where many of William Shakespeare's plays were first performed, caught on fire, no one was hurt. The trousers of a man caught on fire, but his neighbor put the fire out with a bottle of beer. By the way, Mr. Shakespeare was a commoner without a university education. Many people have little respect for people like that, and so they do not believe that Shakespeare wrote the plays attributed to him. Over 4,000 books have been written saying that the "real" author was any of over 57 people, including Queen Elizabeth I. (Of course, Shakespeare wrote the plays attributed to him. Commoners can be intelligent, you know.)[13]

• In Austria, operatic tenor Leo Slezak sometimes heard musical societies play at dances for summer visitors. Often, as the night wore on and the band members became drunker and drunker, the music declined in quality. Once, he saw a band member stuff a sausage into the mouth of a tuba, thus preventing the tuba player from getting any sound at all from his instrument.[14]

• John Steed, the sartorially perfect spy on the TV series *The Avengers*, does a lot of drinking—especially champagne—so of course he has a hangover cure, which we learn in the episode "A Touch of Brimstone." The cure is to play the National Anthem because it "gets you to your feet."[15]

Animals

• Arturo Toscanini once conducted the New York Philharmonic in a Sunday radio broadcast of Beethoven's Ninth Symphony. A flock of canaries was loose in an apartment while the occupant listened to the broadcast. The canaries were silent for the symphony's first three movements, but when the Choral Finale began they flew to the radio, settled on it, and sang with the music. Maestro Toscanini was greatly pleased with this story.[16]

• George White was a producer of revues during the Roaring Twenties. Often, he sat in the ticket office and sold tickets for his revue and was amused whenever someone he had never met demanded good seats because of being "a personal friend of George White's." By the way, Mr. White thought it was a good day when he lost $100,000 at a horse race because he immediately stopped betting on the horses.[17]

• When Tallulah Bankhead appeared with a monkey in *Conchita* at the Queen's Theatre, it did not go well. When the monkey first appeared on stage, it grabbed Tallulah's black wig, then ran away, revealing Tallulah's blond hair. The audience laughed, and Tallulah turned a cartwheel on stage.[18]

Art and Artists

• Joe Greene of Stillwater, Oklahoma, does not like good things to go to waste. In the summer of 2012, he looked in a trashcan outside a church in Stillwater and saw the corner of an old wooden frame. He took it out and looked at it. The glass pane in front was smeared with ketchup and barbeque sauce. He said, "It had been buried in somebody's picnic." He took it and left. For about six weeks, he ignored it, and then he looked at it again. On the back was a photocopied newspaper article about Doel Reed and some contest-entry forms for an arts festival in Taos, New Mexico. From 1924 to 1959, Mr. Reed had worked in the art department at Oklahoma A&M College, which is now Oklahoma State University. In 1967, he created the drawing in the frame. Mr. Greene called a friend who is an artist, and the friend advised him to take the drawing to the art department of Oklahoma State University. Chris Ramsey, the head of the art department, advised him to have the drawing reframed. He did, and the drawing looked brand-new. Mr. Greene then donated the drawing to Oklahoma State University in honor of his wife, Dixie Mosier-Greene, who is part of the university's philosophy department faculty. The drawing is titled "Near Ledoux," and now it hangs in the Oklahoma State University Bartlett Center for the Visual Arts. Oklahoma State University art historian Louise Siddons said about the drawing and its artist, "It's just really direct and clearly drawn. He just communicates how it felt to be in that place in that light." Mr. Greene is proud to have rescued the work of art. He said, "My life is weird. And it gets weirder all the time."[19]

• Rembrandt van Rijn didn't have to worry about models. The people depicted in his *Night Watch* are all people who paid him to be in the painting. Those who paid more got a better position in the painting. By the way, Vincent van Gogh painted 22 portraits of himself. This does not mean that he had a big ego; rather, he was always so broke that he could not afford to hire models to sit for him.[20]

• Landscape artist Joseph Turner (1775-1851) painted his *Peace: Burial at Sea of the Body of Sir David Wilkie*, using some very dark colors for the sails. Clarkson Stanfield objected to the "funereal and unnatural blackness of the sails," but Mr. Turner replied, "I only wish I had any color to make them blacker."[21]

• Peter Bruegel had two sons who also painted, and who acquired the nicknames Hell and Velvet. Peter the Younger painted a lot of devils, so he became known as Hell Bruegel, while Jan painted a lot of rich fabrics, so he became known as Velvet Bruegel.[22]

Audiences

• Choreographer Merce Cunningham wanted people to care about what they were seeing when they watched a dance performance. Frequently, audiences did care when they watched a Merce Cunningham dance performance. In 1964, a Paris audience threw vegetables at the Merce Cunningham dancers. One month later, in Cologne, the audience roared its approval at the dancers. By the way, set designer Robert Rauschenberg was very creative for Mr. Cunningham and his dancers. Once, Mr. Rauschenberg and an assistant ironed their shirts upstage. For another performance, he dyed clothing many colors, and then hung them on the stage to dry, where they dripped into buckets. Also by the way, sometimes servers get in a hurry and speak in shorthand. One harried waitress served food to Cunningham dancers Carolyn Brown and Viola Farber. The waiter said to Ms. Brown, "You're the fried chicken," and to Ms. Farber, "You're the stuffed shrimp."[23]

• A 1991 TV commercial shows a thirsty woman climbing up a mountain to get a bottle of Perrier. When she arrives at the top of the mountain, she comes face to face with a thirsty lion that has climbed up the other side of the mountain. The lion roars at the woman, the woman roars at the lion, and vanquished, the lion slinks off, leaving the woman to enjoy the Perrier. Not everyone liked this commercial. It won the Grand Prize at the Cannes Advertising Festival, but the audience booed as the commercial's director, Jean-Paul Goude, picked up the award. Mr. Goude booed the audience back.[24]

Authors

• Before he became famous, James M. Barrie, author of *Peter Pan*, made the rounds of theatrical producers, asking them to read his plays. By means of a letter of introduction, he persuaded John Hare to read a play, and then he waited outside Mr. Hare's office as he read it. Soon, roars of indignation came from the office, and Mr. Barrie returned to find Mr. Hare jumping up and down on the play—Mr. Barrie's handwriting was so bad that Mr. Hare was unable to read it. Afterward, Mr. Barrie paid other people to make transcripts of his plays.[25]

• Every Christmas Eve, humorist Robert Benchley and his wife read *A Christmas Carol* by Charles Dickens. The parts that made him cry were not the sad parts—but "the parts that are so glad that they shut off your wind." By the way, Mr. Benchley was a great reader, but he did not want to seem pretentious. While in Hollywood, he would sometimes read a volume by Marcel Proust—after first covering it up with a murder mystery dust jacket.[26]

• Antoinette Sibley and Anthony Dowell were ballet partners who thought alike. Shortly after their book, *Sibley and Dowell*, was published, they met in a restaurant. Both were carrying white bags, both were carrying copies of their book, both had thought about not bringing copies of their book, and both made the same apology for bringing copies of their book.[27]

• Anthony Trollope used to get up at 5:30 each morning so that he could write before getting dressed for breakfast. To ensure that he arose at such an early hour, he gave an elderly groom an extra £5 per year to bring him coffee and awaken him. By the way, author J.P. Muller was once asked what advice he would give to would-be writers. He replied, "Don't."[28]

• Professor Charles Townsend Copeland once promised Maxwell Perkins to write his memoirs, but when Mr. Perkins telegraphed him that he would come to Boston to pick up the first few chapters, Professor Copeland telegraphed back that they weren't started yet, so "Come up eight years from now."[29]

Children

• In a 1967 interview with Mary Harrington Hall, Charles Schulz said that his children had given him a total of three lines that he had used in *Peanuts*, his comic strip. At dinner, Amy, his daughter, was talking quite a lot, and Mr. Schulz asked her, "Couldn't you be quiet for just a little while?" Shortly afterward, she was buttering a piece of bread and asked, "Am I buttering too loud for you?" Craig, his son, often had dirty fingernails. One day, they were clean and his parents asked how he had gotten them so clean. Craig answered, "I used toothpaste." And when Monty, another son, was in kindergarten, Mr. Schulz read him a bedtime story and tried to get him to go to sleep, and Monty said that he didn't want to close his eyes. Why? "Because it's dark in there."[30]

• Ballet impresario Sergei Diaghilev paid little attention to time. When the young Alicia Markova was dancing for him, he invited her and her governess out for a ride in the country to see some Spanish dancing and to enjoy tea, but he arrived for the engagement late. Alicia and her governess waited an hour for him, then left, and he arrived an hour after they had left. The next day, young Alicia told him calmly, "You broke your appointment, Sergypop. I know that you are a busy man, but that is no excuse for not turning up when you invite a friend to go out with you." Mr. Diaghilev apologized, then he made a new appointment for the following day, and when Alicia and her governess arrived, he was waiting for them.[31]

• When Sir Harold Wilson, former Prime Minister of England, was a child, he was cast as the Midshipmite in Gilbert and Sullivan's *HMS Pinafore*. One of the benefits of his role was that each night on stage he got a basket of goodies. One night, the basket was filled with especially large candies, and soon he became aware that all eyes were on him—and for good reason. Because of the large size of the piece of candy he had stuck in his mouth, one of his cheeks stuck out much farther than the other.[32]

• Ruth Weisberg decided to become an artist at age six after taking just three classes at the Chicago Art Institute. She remembers telling her parents and she also remembers that they didn't laugh; instead, their reaction was, "Oh, wonderful!" Ruth did not go home immediately after her classes—she preferred to visit the art galleries. In fact, while she was in Italy, she used to put herself to sleep not by counting sleep, but instead by imaginatively visiting the art galleries of her youth.[33]

• Ana Samways writes an entertaining almost-daily humor column for the *New Zealand Herald*. Rhys Haman of Tauranga sent her this anecdote about his niece's birthday. Her four-year-old daughter, Naeva, gave her a little box in which were some pieces of fluff. Mr. Haman wrote about Naeva, "She said it was some bits of cloud, and she and her brother Kobe had climbed up high in the sky to get it for her! Not many people can say that they got a piece of cloud for their birthday."[34]

• Here are two anecdotes about children: 1) During church, a young boy threw his quarter at the collection plate, but missed, and the quarter fell to the floor, making a loud racket. Another young boy, who had watched the throwing attempt, said loudly, "Air ball!" 2) An elderly man was known for saying long prayers to close the church service. Once, a three-year-old girl got impatient, so she yelled "AMEN!" The elderly man quickly ended his prayer.[35]

• As a boy, jazz giant Duke Ellington had read about the sinking of the *Titanic*, so when he sailed to Europe the first time, he stayed up all the first night to look out for icebergs. By the way, the adult Mr. Ellington was married to a jealous, knife-wielding woman named Edna, who once gave him a permanent scar by slashing his face.[36]

Choreographers

• When Anton Dolin's first choreographed his "Doll Ballet," lots of people came to him, requesting something special, such as a solo for a friend. He listened to them—as he says, "like a fool"—with the result that the ballet was very bad, and he had to re-choreograph it, with no special bits, but instead with all the dancers used *en masse*. By the way, in 1917, when he was a young man (and still dancing under his real name: Patrick Kay), Mr. Dolin appeared in *Fédora*, where he had a small but important role as a Russian page. Sir Squire Bancroft asked him at a rehearsal whether he spoke French. Mr. Dolin replied that he did not; nevertheless, Sir Squire Bancroft asked him to speak the word "madame" as the French do. Mr. Dolin made the attempt, then Sir Squire Bancroft told him, "My lad, you'd better say it in English. Don't try to speak like a Frenchman."[37]

• Choreographer George Balanchine always wanted the members of his New York City Ballet to behave with consideration in whatever place they visited. Once he became very annoyed in West Berlin when some members of his company boarded a bus after carrying out from a restaurant some china cups filled with coffee. By the way, Mr. Balanchine once choreographed a ballet with the title "Pamtgg," which stood for the advertising slogan "Pan Am makes the going great." Unfortunately, the ballet was a flop.[38]

• When choreographer Leonide Massine owned the island of Li Galli, occasionally tourists would try to land on his island. When that happened, Mr. Massine would take a bullhorn and shout at them: "Get off my property." Later, when Rudolf Nureyev owned the island, he would do the same thing.[39]

Clothing

• Stella Ehrhart, age eight in 2012 and then a third-grader at Dundee Elementary School in Omaha, Nebraska, wore costumes to school, beginning when she was in the second grade. That school year, she wore a different costume each school day, but in the third grade she repeated some costumes. She and her mother kept a list of Stella's costumes. On her first day of the second grade, she wore ordinary clothing, but on the second day of school, she dressed as author Laura Ingalls Wilde. The costumes usually featured a notable woman from her book *100 Most Important Women of the 20th Century*, which is heavily illustrated with photographs. The costumes were not necessarily elaborate. She has been singer Billie Holiday (a black dress and a red tissue-paper flower) and actress Grace Kelly (pink satin lace) and Burmese opposition leader Aung San Suu Kyi (a hat that her aunt bought for her in Vietnam). She has also worn costumes such as one for singer Joan Baez (a military-green fitted half-blazer, a patterned blouse, black slacks, and cowboy boots). Classmate Abby Adams identified her favorite of Stella's costumes: "Ummm, Laura Ingalls Wilder. She wore, like, these shoes that were black and white. She wore, like, this dress with leggings. It's kind of cool. I might do it next year." Best friend Virginia Holtzclaw said, "My favorite costume was last year—she dressed as me." Jack Jenowe said, "One time she dressed as our principal. It's cool." Stella's father is actor-director-teacher Kevin Ehrhart, who played the Cat in the Hat during a Rose Theater production of *Seussical the Musical*—Stella played a baby kangaroo. Her mother is actor-director Stephanie Anderson. Her mother liked it when Stella wore a costume for artist "Georgia O'Keeffe. That was one of my favorites." Stella once pointed to a picture of Supreme Court Justice Sandra Day O'Connor and asked, "Mom, was I her on Friday?" Her mother replied, "No. You were Queen Elizabeth."[40]

• Marie Camargo (1710-1770) was an innovator in ballet. Before Ms. Camargo, ballerinas danced in ankle-length skirts. Ms. Camargo caused a scandal by dancing in skirts that showed part of her calf; however, this allowed her to create ballet moves that featured the ballerinas' feet—she was the likely inventor of the *entrechat-quatre*, a move in which the ballerina jumps and crosses her feet four times while in the air. Later, Marie Sallé (1707-1756) further improved the ballerina's clothing by dancing in a petticoat and a simple dress—although she still wore a corset. Today, classical ballerinas dance in tights and a short skirt known as a tutu. By the way, Ms. Camargo knew how to seize opportunity. A mere member of a dance ensemble, she wished to be a star. At a concert, a male dancer named Dumoulin failed to respond to his cue, so Ms. Camargo left the ensemble, went to the front of the stage, and improvised a solo that was enthusiastically applauded. Also by the way, on 14 February 1734, Ms. Sallé produced and starred in *Pygmalion*, which she also choreographed. *Pygmalion* was the first ballet to be fully choreographed by a woman.[41]

• Ballet dancers started out by wearing ankle-length dresses, but the nature of dancing demands that the dancer's form be revealed and as time went on, the dancer's skirt became shorter and shorter until dancers began to wear tutus—the shortest possible skirts. Such shortening of the skirts has been alarming to many. When Marie Camargo first wore a skirt that bared her ankles, authorities made her wear *calçons de précaution*—translated as "precautionary panties," this was an undergarment worn over hose—to protect the audience from accidentally seeing the bare flesh above a stocking. By the way, the great ballet dancer Marie Taglioni is shown in many lithographs wearing a choker around her neck and pearl bracelets on her arms—no matter what role she was dancing. The reason for this consistent costuming is that she had a very long neck and very long arms and the choker and the bracelets helped break up their length.[42]

• Frank Rodney, a British theatrical romantic lead in the late 19th century, was very attached to a dirty tweed cap and an old coat. This upset actress Constance Benson, so she warned him that if he ever again appeared in public wearing those articles of clothing, she would fix them so that not even he would wear them. Mr. Rodney did appear in public wearing them, so Ms. Benson tossed his cap into the fire, then used a penknife to slit his coat down the back. Mr. Rodney rescued his cap from the fire and paid a tailor to sew up his coat, then he continued to wear them. By the way, as long as Mr. Rodney was on stage dressed in his costume and wearing a wig, he looked dashing, but off stage and dressed in his usually unkempt clothing, he looked quite ordinary. Often, a woman in the audience would see him on stage and fall in love with him, then go backstage, and burst into tears with disappointment when she saw what he looked like in real life.[43]

• Ballerina Alicia Markova had very small hands and feet. During a bitterly cold winter, the Ballet Russe de Monte Carlo toured Chicago, where Ms. Markova was forced to keep her hands warm with little girls' Shirley Temple gloves because nothing else would fit her. By the way, small decisions early can make enormous differences later. Ms. Markova was thought to have weak feet and legs when she was a little girl, so her doctor suggested that she study classical ballet to strengthen her limbs. As all of the dance world knows, Ms. Markova became an accomplished ballerina as an adult.[44]

• At the beginning of a long tour, Anna Pavlova took along a huge number of ballet shoes. She would try them all on, quickly reject many of them as unsuitable for her feet, then give them to the members of her company. By the way, Ms. Pavlova loved to swim, although she was not very good at it. She liked to dive into the water and once knocked herself out with a dive.[45]

• Laurence Olivier wore a different suit each day at rehearsals of *Mary Queen of Scots*. This caused resentment among members of the cast and crew, who thought Mr. Olivier was showing off—until he explained, "Each suit is a relic of a different flop."[46]

Comedians and Humorists

• Here are a few anecdotes about comedians: 1) At age 10, comedian Joe Cook got his first job in show business by using a photograph of himself juggling 17 balls. The photograph was faked—the balls were hung from the ceiling with invisible wires. 2) Comedian Eddie Cantor grew up in the city and believed that oranges grew underground. When he went to California and saw his first orange tree, he thought that his friend Georgie Jessel was trying to pull a practical joke by tying the oranges to the tree. 3) Way back in 1929, comedian W.C. Fields used to say that his favorite actor was Benito Mussolini.[47]

• When Corey Ford wrote for *Life* magazine, he worried because a writer named Torrey Ford was also contributing to the magazine. Robert Benchley advised, "Maybe the best idea would be to let Torrey handle the articles, and you handle the checks." By the way, Mr. Benchley once was granted a loan by a bank. The next day, he went to the bank and withdrew all his money, saying, "I don't trust a bank that would lend money to such a poor risk." Also by the way, Mr. Benchley frequently endorsed his checks in strange ways—for example, "Dear Bankers Trust, I love you. Bob."[48]

• As a five-year-old child, Sid Caesar learned several words in foreign languages while helping out in his father's restaurant. Many people of different ethnic groups came in, and they took great delight in teasing young Sid. The Italians would teach him a dirty word in

Russian and send him over to the Russians' table to say it, and then the Russians would teach him a dirty word in Italian and send him over to the Italians' table to say it. This training in languages was of enormous help when Mr. Caesar began to speak foreign-sounding gibberish on his TV shows.[49]

• Frank Aloysius Robert Tinney became a comedian in the early 20th century and stumbled upon his act almost by accident. One day, he was called upon to perform without his partner, so he was forced to use a badly rehearsed orchestra leader as his partner, and of course the orchestra leader muffed his lines. This made Mr. Tinney angry, so on stage he began to berate the orchestra leader: "Say, you're crabbing my act. You hadn't ought to of said that. You ought to of said ...." The audience felt that this was hilarious.[50]

• Helen Traubel, who was a somewhat large woman and a very fine singer, and Groucho Marx once appeared in Gilbert and Sullivan's *Mikado* together. One day, Ms. Traubel arrived late for rehearsal and Groucho told her, "Hello, Helen, pull up a couple of chairs and sit down."[51]

Chapter 2: From Comic Strips to Education

Comic Strips

• In 1974, Charles M. Schulz, the creator of the comic strip *Peanuts*, was the Grand Marshall of the Rose Parade. His *Peanuts* comic strip of that time contains an in-joke: Linus walks into a room in which Lucy is watching the Rose Parade and asks, "Has the Grand Marshall gone by yet?" Lucy replies, "Yeah, you missed him ... but he wasn't anyone you ever heard of." In one early cartoon, Charlie Brown worries that no one cares about him, and then he says, "I'll bet that Doctor Spock cares about me." Shortly afterward, Mr. Schulz received a letter from Doctor Benjamin Spock, author of a famous child-care book. The letter stated, "You can tell Charlie Brown that I care about him very much." By the way, Mr. Schulz once said, "Cartooning is a *fairly* sort of proposition. You have to be fairly intelligent—if you were really intelligent, you'd be doing something else. You have to draw fairly well—if you drew really well, you'd be a painter. You have to write fairly well—if you wrote really well, you'd be writing books. It's great for a fairly person like me."[52]

Conductors

• Oscar Levant told these stories about conductors: 1) Leopold Stokowski was acting as a guest conductor with the New York Philharmonic when he was annoyed by a musician who talked during a rehearsal. Maestro Stokowski ordered the musician to leave the rehearsal, but instead of being contrite, the musician said, "Thank you—I haven't had a Thursday evening off all winter." 2) Conductor Modest Altschuler of the Russian Symphony Orchestra once tried to get a more emotional performance from an oboist during a rehearsal of *Scheherazade* by pointing to the concertmaster and saying, "Here is the princess and you are making love to her." Maestro Altschuler then stopped and looked at the poor complexion of the concertmaster, and added, "I'm sorry I can't do better." 3) Walter Damrosch was known for conducting with a slow beat. Once, a member of his orchestra threatened him, "If you bawl me out again, I'll follow your beat." 4) A musician who continually tuned his violin during each pause in a rehearsal annoyed Arturo Toscanini, who told the violinist, "It's not the A that counts, but the B."[53]

• Arturo Toscanini made his debut as a conductor when he was 19 years old. He was a cellist in an orchestra traveling in South America, and in Rio de Janeiro the regular music conductor got into an argument with the manager. Because a conductor was needed for *Aida*, and because Toscanini was already known for his musical ability, he took over and conducted despite not having time for even one rehearsal—he even conducted from memory. The performance was electrifying, and a new star was recognized. By the way, Maestro Toscanini's ears were very sensitive. Once, he listened to a broadcast by another conductor and was so upset that he knelt and begged, "Please, please! No more *ritenuti*!" Also by the way, while on tour in Rio de Janeiro, one of Maestro Toscanini's violinists was killed by an autobus. Toscanini wept, created a fund for the violinist's widow, and made a big contribution.[54]

• Arturo Toscanini had a phenomenal memory and conducted without a score—but he had a good reason for doing so. His eyesight was not very good, and to see the notes he would have had to bring his eyes very close to the score, so a score was useless to him while conducting. After Toscanini began to conduct without a score, other conductors began to imitate him in a pretentious way—at the beginning of a performance, some conductors would walk to the conductor's podium, close the opened score, then begin to conduct. Horn player Harold Meek of the Boston Symphony Orchestra believes that many conductors would benefit from having a score in front of them, as did such fine conductors as Serge Koussevitzky and Sir Georg Solti.[55]

• Conductor Serge Koussevitzky used to take classical music to parts of Russia where classical music—and its instruments—had not been heard before. One farmer was fascinated by the trombone, and at the conclusion of a concert, thinking that the musician had been trying to disassemble the trombone—and not succeeding—the farmer took the trombone and used his great strength to break the trombone apart. The farmer then handed the pieces of the ruined trombone to the astonished musician and said, "There you are, sir."[56]

• Gianandrea Gavazzeni once conducted *Un ballo in maschera*, in which Plácido Domingo sang. Mr. Domingo sang the lines "Amelia! *tu m'ami?*"—and the orchestra came in full blast. People complained that with the full orchestra, they could not hear Mr. Domingo and his Amelia, but Mr. Gavazzeni said, "It doesn't matter! That's the way Verdi wanted it!" Thereafter, whenever the full orchestra came in, Mr. Domingo didn't sing, but merely mouthed the words, knowing that no one could hear him anyway.[57]

• As a young conductor, Thomas Beecham gathered together a small orchestra of fine, spirited, young players. They did a lot of traveling by train in the north of England, and each time they arrived at Preston Junction, they lit fireworks. Because of this habit, they became known as "The Fireworks Orchestra of Lancashire." By the way, Sir Thomas could be an exacting conductor. To record the first four minutes of the "William Tell Overture" took him and his orchestra three hours. Afterward, Sir Thomas treated the five hard-working cellists to champagne.[58]

• Not all conductors like applause—at least not while they are conducting. Sir Thomas Beecham once told an audience at Covent Garden, "Shut up," because he felt the audience's applause was intrusive. Afterward, there was dead silence—for months—whenever Sir Thomas conducted at Covent Garden. The silence got to Sir Thomas after a while, and he once told the orchestra after he had mounted the rostrum, "Ladies and gentlemen, let us pray."[59]

• During the Roaring Twenties, Arturo Toscanini was the musical director of the New York Philharmonic; however, his suite at the Astor Hotel was very modest. In fact, there was a large blinking advertising sign outside his window. Fortunately, this didn't bother Mr. Toscanini—he enjoyed watching the sign blink on and off.[60]

• Sir Thomas Beecham had such a fabulous memory for scores that he didn't always need to prepare assiduously before conducting an opera. Once, he stood before the podium, then was forced to ask, "By the way, which opera are we giving tonight?" After hearing the answer, he conducted the opera masterfully.[61]

• When Mary Garden became director of the Chicago Grand Opera Company, she wanted Giorgio Polacco as conductor. Therefore, she sent Mr. Polacco a telegram asking him to be her musical director, and he cabled back, "I'M SAILING"—without even first asking what his salary would be.[62]

Conversation

• On 7 August 2012, three teenagers—Alexa Erb, age 18; Victoria Cornell, age 19; and Claude Mumbere, age 18—sat on Church Street in Burlington, Vermont, for three hours and paid $1 to strangers to tell them their stories. The three teenagers called out compliments to passersby and held this sign: "Tell us your story and we'll give you a dollar." They had $26, and they spent $15. The stories were about Cambodia, Afghanistan, homelessness, and mental illness—and many more topics, too. Ms. Erb said, "I have found that sometimes listening means you don't need to give a response. Just knowing that someone is truly listening to what you are saying is sometimes enough." Ms. Cornell said, "I see now how we can use our stories, and our brokenness, to create bonds. We are all equal in our human condition; even when we are broken, we can become whole through sharing." Mr. Mumbere said, "We have heard many stories today. Even from people who think they don't have a story. When they start talking, there is so much to be said. It's amazing to see what you can find in someone when you just take the time to listen." Ms. Cornell said, "The common theme is that life is going to suck at times, but beauty always comes from the pain somehow. If you're willing to pay it forward, and listen to someone's story, it will be worth it."[63]

• A man claimed to be a Zen Buddhist and Master of Silence. Although he seldom spoke, he had two disciples who were very eloquent. One day, a Pilgrim visited the Master of Silence in the temple while the disciples were absent. The Pilgrim asked, "What is the Buddha?" The Master of Silence did not speak, but instead looked all around for his disciples. The Pilgrim asked other questions, all of which were met by silence and the Master's looking around for his disciples, then he thanked the Master of Silence and left. Outside the temple, the Pilgrim met the Master's two disciples, who asked how the audience had gone. The Pilgrim was enthusiastic: "When I asked him what Buddha is, he turned his face in all directions, implying that human beings are always looking for the Buddha, but actually the Buddha is not to be sought in such a way. And his answers to my other questions were even more impressive—what a remarkable master!" The two disciples then said goodbye to the Pilgrim and went in to see the Master of Silence, who told them, "Where have you been? Some crazy Pilgrim has been driving me mad with impossible questions!"[64]

• Dr. Samuel Johnson did not tolerate fools for very long. At a dinner, someone asked him many personal questions, while volunteering personal information about himself. Dr. Johnson stood it as long as he could, then said, "Sir, you have but two topics: yourself and me. I am sick of both." On another occasion, a bore sat next to Dr. Johnson and remarked that there were many reasons for drinking to excess. In making his argument, he said, "Drinking drives away care and makes us forget whatever is disagreeable. Would you not allow a man to drink for that reason?" Dr. Johnson replied, "Yes, sir—if he sat next to you." By the way, James Boswell once asked Dr. Johnson whether good cooks were more essential than good poets. Dr. Johnson replied, "I don't suppose that there is a dog in town but what thinks so."[65]

• Giovanni Antonio Bazzi, nicknamed Sodoma (1477-1549), who apparently enjoyed shocking people, once listed the inhabitants of his house as follows: "Item an owl to frighten witches, two peacocks, two dogs, two cats, a sparrow-hawk and other birds of prey, six fowls, eighteen chicks, two moor fowl and many other birds; to name all of which would only cause confusion. I have, besides these, three abominably wicked beasts, to wit, my three women." By the way, Henry Fuseli (1741-1823) once was bored by the conversation of some guests, so he suddenly exclaimed, "We had pork for dinner today." This surprised his guests, one of whom said, "Mr. Fuseli! What an odd remark!" Mr. Fuseli replied, "Why, it is as good as anything you have been saying for the last half-hour."[66]

• Mr. Justice Hawkins (1817-1907) enjoyed attending the races. While sitting as judge, Mr. Hawkins saw a prisoner say something to a constable, and he asked the constable what the prisoner had said. The constable replied, "I—I would rather not say, your lordship." However, Mr. Hawkins insisted, and the constable said, "He asked me, your lordship, who that heathen with the sheepskin was, as he had often seen him at the racecourse."[67]

Critics

• Francis Hodgson Burnett, author of *Little Lord Fauntleroy*, started a fashion trend for little boys, whom parents made wear black velvet suits with lace; the little boys also had long, curled hair. When, years later, she started to get bad reviews of her books, people speculated that the bad reviews were written by these little boys, who had grown up and wanted revenge. By the way, as a critic, Edgar Allen Poe was merciless, whether criticizing one writer or an entire group of writers. About the writing community in Boston, Massachusetts, he wrote, "Their pumpkin pies are delicious. Their poetry is not so good."[68]

• Charles Lamb's play *Mr. H* was a dismal failure, with the audience hissing it throughout its performance. According to legend, Mr. Lamb, who was in the audience, joined in the hissing so that no one would think he had written the play. By the way, after the opening-night performance of his play *Home Chat*, Noel Coward came forward to take a bow. A voice from the audience called out, "We expected better." Mr. Coward replied, "So did I."[69]

• *Boston Transcript* critic Henry Taylor Parker signed his articles H.T.P., which the victims of his criticism said stood for "Hell To Pay." Once, some talkative members of the audience bore the brunt of his wit. He told them, "Those people up on the stage are making so much noise I can't hear a word you're saying."[70]

• Jerome K. Jerome (1859-1927) noticed something odd about the critics who reviewed his books. When they reviewed his first book, they denounced it as "rubbish." However, when they reviewed his second book, they denounced it as an unworthy successor to his first book, which had been excellent.[71]

Dance

• Choreographer Merce Cunningham once won a prize at an international festival in Paris. Oddly, and without Mr. Cunningham's permission, a representative of the State Department of the United States picked up the prize, despite not having supported Mr. Cunningham financially. Several weeks later, the State Department mailed the prize to Mr. Cunningham—in a package on which there was postage due! By the way, a college student writing an M.A. thesis once wrote the very busy Mr. Cunningham and asked him to write her about his technique. Mr. Cunningham's reply: "Tell her to come study!" Also by the way, in dance class or rehearsals, Mr. Cunningham would sometimes be asked how to do a certain move. He always replied, "You just do it."[72]

• In vaudeville, audiences grew to know and love successful acts. This sometimes created problems. For example, the act might be a tap dancing act, whose members wanted to change the act when they grew tired of it. However, the audience wanted to see the same dance they had seen the last time the tap dancing act had gone through their town. For example, the Berry Brothers were famous for their cane dance and danced it for decades. Warren Berry once said, "I was so tired of hearing that music. ... I would stand in the wings before going onstage, and just grit my teeth every time." However, if the tap dancers ever wanted to change their act, their agent would tell them they wouldn't be able to be booked.[73]

• Choreographer Agnes de Mille was once asked if she had a dance prepared that could be performed by the Ballet Russe de Monte Carlo. She replied, "Certainly, I'll go home and get it." Actually, she didn't have the dance already prepared—she went home and created one. By the way, at age five, Agnes started taking piano lessons. Later, she said that she had learned to read music before she had learned to read words. And at age 13, Agnes saw Anna Pavlova dance. From that time, she knew that she wanted to devote her life to dance. She said later, "I was as clearly marked as though she had looked me in the face and called my name."[74]

• Suzanne Farrell learned that she was to dance the role of Dulcinea in George Balanchine's new work *Don Quixote*, so she started to read the work by Cervantes, but after 400 pages, Dulcinea still had not appeared in the book, although the Don did describe her appearance frequently. When Ms. Farrell told Mr. Balanchine that she found reading *Don Quixote* "rather overwhelming, philosophically and otherwise," he told her, "Don't worry, dear, you don't need to read it." Of course, as the choreographer of the ballet, Mr. Balanchine was able to tell her what she needed to know to dance the role.[75]

• Ballerina Alicia Markova became a celebrity when she danced *Giselle* in New York. During the performance, her foot was broken, but she continued dancing. Ms. Markova once told Agnes de Mille, "I continued the whole solo variation, little hops on pointe and all. Think of it: right across the stage on one toe on a fractured foot." By the way, ballet shoes last for only one performance, but they can be worth the expense. After each performance, Ms. Markova had to be cut out of her shoes. However, after each performance, four men had to help carry the bouquets of flowers she received.[76]

• When George Balanchine and Alexandra Danilova were keeping house together and working for Sergei Diaghilev, they participated in the Monte Carlo premiere of *Le Bal*. Unfortunately, all of the soloists except Ms. Danilova received flowers at the curtain. This made Mr. Diaghilev angry, and he spoke to Mr. Balanchine about it. At the next performance, Mr. Balanchine sent Ms. Danilova 100 roses at the curtain—there were so many that she couldn't carry them all, and she gave many of them away to other members of the company.[77]

• Early in his career, ballet master George Balanchine was a dancer, although he preferred choreographing. Nevertheless, as a young dancer he showed great stamina. Once, he missed a train, chased after it, failed to catch up with it, and so was forced to bicycle 16 miles to his next performance, where he danced a *pas de deux*. By the way, Mr. Balanchine's "Stars and Stripes" was so popular with audiences that he called it an "applause machine." Also by the way, when the American — but internationally famous — Mr. Balanchine learned that President Ronald Reagan had chosen him to be the recipient of the highest award an American citizen can receive—the Medal of Freedom, he joked, "Of what country?"[78]

• George Balanchine used real life when he choreographed his "Serenade" to Tchaikovsky's "Serenade in C for String Orchestra." A ballerina once arrived late for rehearsal, so "Serenade" includes a ballerina entering the dance late. A male dancer became available suddenly, so Mr. Balanchine included a male dancer in "Serenade."

During rehearsal, an exhausted and overwhelmed dancer collapsed to the floor, so in "Serenade" the ballerina falls to the floor.[79]

• Ballerina Margot Fonteyn's husband was involved in planning a political coup in Panama. Once, Ms. Fonteyn found a box of grenades in her basement—she was not surprised. Ms. Fonteyn often danced witrh Rudolf Nureyev, At the Kirov School for Ballet, a very young Rudolf was told by a teacher, "Young man, you will either become a brilliant dancer or a total failure—and most likely you will be a failure."[80]

• Sallie Wilson used to be a principal dancer for American Ballet Theatre. She began to study dance through an accident. A musician, she was playing in a school orchestra during a ballet performance when the lights in the orchestra pit went out. This meant she had to play from memory, and instead of looking at the music, she was able to watch the ballet performance. She liked what she saw, so she began to study ballet.[81]

• When Ted Shawn was attending college in Denver in the early part of the 20th century, dancing was not permitted; however, Mr. Shawn and his fraternity brothers wanted to hold dances. Therefore, they sent out invitations that said, "You're invited to come and play folk games with us to music on a slick floor."[82]

• Dancing in South America has its advantages, as flowers are inexpensive and plentiful. After a performance of *Giselle*, ballerina Alicia Markova was presented with a giant basket of white camellias. She and the *corps de ballet* were so astonished by its size that they counted the blooms—500![83]

• Dancers Irina Baronova and George Skibine used to play a childish (and for dancers, dangerous) game while waiting to go on stage to perform—they would have a contest to see who could stamp on the other's foot first.[84]

Death

• The elderly actor A.E. Matthews once took a nap in his dressing room while sitting on a chair. During his nap, he fell off the chair, landed on the floor, and continued his nap there. The call boy found him on the floor, was frightened, and told the stage manager, "Mr. Matthews is dead." Before anything could be done, Mr. Matthews woke up and went out on stage and performed very well as usual. Later, he told the call boy, "Next time you find me dead on the floor I suggest you tell them, 'I *think* Mr. Matthews is dead.'"[85]

• Theatrical director Tyrone Guthrie had a heart attack and was in an oxygen tent. One of his aunts thought that he was dead and opened the oxygen tent to look in. Mr. Guthrie opened one eye and said, "Not dead yet, fiddle dee-dee." By the way, despite being very busy, Mr. Guthrie was very willing to give his time to others. His wife, Judy, once said that if the Timbuctoo Ladies Guild ever wanted him to give them a talk, Mr. Guthrie would write them: "Delighted! Can fit you in nicely on Thursday, on my way from Minneapolis to Belfast."[86]

• The great dancer Bill Robinson, aka Mr. Bojangles, was afraid to fly. People told him that when it was his day to die, it wouldn't matter whether he was up in the air or down on the ground, but he responded, "I don't plan to be up there on the pilot's day." By the way, at one time Mr. Bojangles wasn't getting along with Ethel Waters, so he taught his dog to perform a trick. Whenever anyone said "Ethel Waters" to the dog, the dog growled.[87]

• Pianist Franz Reizenstein once performed Beethoven's *Emperor Concerto* with an orchestra conducted by Josef Krips. Unfortunately, Mr. Reizenstein made mistakes, both during rehearsal and during the concert. After the concert, he asked Mr. Krips, "Well, what do you think of me now, Josef?" Mr. Krips replied, "The trouble is this, my friend. There are always witnesses to a musical murder."[88]

• When Serge Diaghilev died, Anton Dolin saw his photograph in a newspaper and without reading the article, knew immediately what it meant. He went to Lydia Lopokova and George Balanchine crying,

"Serge Pavlovich *est mort*." However, they were at least able to take comfort because Mr. Diaghilev had died in Venice, where he had always hoped he would die.[89]

Education

• When Alicia Markova, whose name at birth was Alicia Marks, was a young ballet student, she saw the great Russian dancer Anna Pavlova, and afterwards wanted to meet her. Her father went backstage, met Ms. Pavlova's husband, and explained that his daughter wanted to meet Ms. Pavlova. Monsieur Dandré, Ms. Pavlova's husband, asked who his daughter was. Not wishing to lie, but also not wishing to admit that his daughter was only eight years old, Mr. Marks replied, "She is a young dancer who has already attracted the attention of the critics." (Mr. Marks' statement was true, as little Alicia had danced a little on the stage and had been briefly mentioned in a press notice.) Hearing that the critics had noticed Mr. Marks' young daughter, M. Dandré set up an appointment for her to meet the great Pavlova the following day. This is Anna Pavlova's advice to eight-year-old dance student Alicia Markova: "You must realize that your life will be all work, lots and lots of hard work, and unless you are prepared to face that and give up your pleasures in order to be a dancer, it is better that you decide now to do something else. You must not be misled when you go to the theater and see a ballerina cheered as she takes her call with her arms full of roses. That is just a fleeting moment of compensation in a life that is nothing but continuous work until the day you retire."[90]

• Some student hacks (pranks) at MIT involve the classroom. On 25 October 1985, students arrived for a physics lecture. On their way into the classroom, they picked up what they thought were class handouts, but one of the handouts was hacked. It was an assignment sheet, and the assignment was to create a paper airplane. Following the instructions on the hacked assignment sheet, the students made paper airplanes and at exactly 11:15 a.m. launched hundreds of airplanes at the professor. Here are some other notable hacks: 1) In 1949, students who were taking a class early Saturday morning showed up wearing pajamas and robes. 2) In 1978, a student who was going to take a final exam spread a tablecloth over his desk and then placed on it a corkscrew, three bottles of wine, some cheese and bread, and his regulation No. 2 pencils. 3) In 1982, students reversed every desk in a lecture room so that instead of facing the front of the room (and the chalkboard), they faced the back of the room. This hack took much work because every desk was bolted to the floor.[91]

• Tyler Cowen is a professor of economics at George Mason University. Alex Tabarrok remembers, "Tyler once walked into class the day of the final exam and he said, 'Here is the exam. Write your own questions. Write your own answers. Harder questions and better answers get more points.' Then he walked out." In a 13 August 2012 comment on this blog entry, Ragbatz wrote, "In the 1960's a Harvard chemistry professor posed a question on a chemistry final examination along these lines: '10% Extra Credit. Write a question to be used as an extra credit question on a final examination in chemistry. The ideal extra credit question should be worth about 10% of the grade on the examination as a whole, and test facility with the material covered during the course.' My friend Tom Hervey received full credit with the following answer: '10% Extra Credit. Write a question to be used as an extra credit question on a final examination in chemistry. The ideal extra credit question should be worth about 10% of the grade on the examination as a whole, and test facility with the material covered during the course.'"[92]

• When Natalia Makarova was a young ballet dancer in the Soviet Union, she fell while rehearsing *Cinderella*, knocking the wind out of herself so badly that she couldn't cry out although she had dislocated her shoulder. Later, as Antonina Ivanovna, the company masseuse, was putting her bones back in their proper place, young Natalia cried out. Her teacher, Natalia Mikhailovna Dudinskaya, a virtuoso dancer turned teacher, heard her, so she came in and talked to her, saying,

"Don't worry, everything will be all right. You'll be on stage in three or four days. We, too, frequently danced in pain and hurt. It's nothing. As you see, we made it." This may seem callous, but later Ms. Makarova realized that her teacher was right. One of the things that she learned from Ms. Dudinskaya was how to "triumph over the body."[93]

• Zen master Busshin was once asked by a monk, "Do heaven and hell exist?" Busshin answered, "No." Overhearing Busshin, some samurai, who were generous benefactors of the temple and who were amazed by his answer, asked him the same question: "Do heaven and hell exist?" This time Busshin answered, "Yes." The samurai then asked Busshin why he was being contradictory. Busshin replied, "If I tell you there's neither heaven nor hell, where would the alms come from?" By the way, Zuigan, the Chinese Zen master, used to wake up every morning and have this conversation with himself: "Master? ... Yes, sir! ... Be wide awake! ... Yes, sir! ... And from now on don't let anyone deceive you! ... Yes, sir! Yes, sir!"[94]

• Maestro Serge Koussevitzky had enormous control over the Boston Symphony Orchestra. He had the final say over who would be the guest conductors during his rare breaks, and he had final say over the programs they would conduct. Whenever a guest conductor submitted a program that included a work by Tchaikovsky, Maestro Koussevitzky would delete that work from the program—the only conductor allowed to perform Tchaikovsky with the Boston Symphony Orchestra was himself. By the way, maestro Koussevitzky, who was born in Russia, occasionally gave conducting classes, at one of which he made a famous remark: "Fine, fine, that's awful."[95]

• White is the color of innocence. Someone just beginning to study a martial art wears a white belt. In time, and with much use, the belt becomes darker and darker, almost black. Later, with much more use, the belt frays and grows light in color again, signifying a return to innocence—something much prized in Zen. By the way, you can learn by teaching. This is well understood in the martial arts—the dojo, the place where the martial arts are taught and practiced, is known traditionally as the "Place of Enlightenment." Also by the way, Bernie Bernheim began to study karate when he was 57. At the age of 61, he earned his black belt.[96]

• Geoff Edwards, who now lives in Whangarei, New Zealand, was a 13-year-old student in London in 1953—when teachers were strict and often gave as punishment a whack with a cane on a student's left hand. He remembers, "John Smith often got a whack. One day in a science lesson on gravity, John kept dropping things on the floor, laughing, and blaming gravity. The teacher, who was also our sports teacher, opened the window, grabbed Smith from his seat and dangled him head-first out of the second-storey window, holding him by the ankles. Then he shouted, 'Now, Smith, do you understand the GRAVITY of the situation?'"[97]

• As a teenager, future ballerina Patricia Bowman took lessons from the great choreographer Michel Fokine. She says that he taught in percentages. For example, she would hold her leg in a certain position, and he might say, "Your leg is only 35 percent. Could I have maybe 65?" Or he might say, "That's very good, but could I have 100 percent?" By the way, dancers sometimes resort to odd ways of making money. Lar Lubovitch, a dancer and choreographer of note, worked early in his career as a go-go dancer at Trude Heller's Greenwich Village nightclub. He danced on a narrow ledge and held onto a doorknob for balance.[98]

• Isaac Stern brought the child prodigy Itzhak Perlman, a violinist, to the attention of agent Sol Hurok. Itzhak was only 12 years old and had been crippled by polio, so Mr. Hurok wondered if he could ever be a success. Mr. Stern replied, "If you risk it, you'll pay for his lessons and his fiddle and give him $500 a week for two years. He will play six concerts a year, not more. He'll study. In two years you'll make a new contract, mutually agreeable. In five years he will be worth a fortune."

Mr. Hurok took Mr. Stern's advice, and young Itzhak turned out to be the success Mr. Stern had predicted.[99]

• As a teenager, Charles MacArthur attended the Wilson Memorial Academy, whose yearbook showed his photograph and a blank space normally reserved for the listing of accomplishments of the person in the photograph—Glee Club, Spanish Club, 4-H Club, Member of the Wrestling Team, etc. After Mr. MacArthur became a successful playwright and screenwriter, he went back to the academy, where he was invited to fill in the space in the yearbook. He wrote, "Pres. Late Sleepers Club; Trustee: Bar Companions (a Pub); Editor: Who's Who (a Humor Sheet)."[100]

• Mathilde Marchesi, the voice teacher of Francis Alda, could be temperamental. Once, she angrily told Ms. Alda to leave at once: "And don't come back. I will teach you no more." Ms. Alda believed her, but the following afternoon Ms. Marchesi's valet stopped by Ms. Alda's apartment to ask her why she hadn't shown up for her usual morning voice lesson.[101]

Chapter 3: From Fans to Mishaps

Fans

• Russell Johnson has many fans because he played the Professor on *Gilligan's Island*. Once, a fan asked for a special autograph, saying that he wanted him to write, "Thanks for saving my life in 'Nam." Because this made Mr. Russell laugh, he wrote the autograph exactly as requested. Dawn Wells, who played Mary Ann on *Gilligan's Island*, also has many fans. Once, she boarded an airplane and all the passengers sang the theme song from *Gilligan's Island*. On another occasion, she was touring a castle in Bavaria and some fans came running up to her, crying, "Mary Ann! Mary Ann!"[102]

• Customs vary from culture to culture. While Alexandra Danilova and Alicia Markova were dancing in Rio de Janeiro, fans would wait by the stage door after the performance. To show their appreciation for a fine performance, the fans threw firecrackers at the ballet dancers' feet. By the way, in Monte Carlo, Ms. Danilova and George Balanchine stayed in a room next door to that of world-famous pianist Vladimir Horowitz. Each morning, they were awakened by Mr. Horowitz' playing of Liszt's "*Valse Oubliée*."[103]

• While appearing in *Charlot's Revue* in New York City, both Gertrude Lawrence and Beatrice Lillie scored notable successes. When the show finally closed in 1924, Ms. Lawrence and Ms. Lillie left the theater only to discover that some of their more enthusiastic admirers were sitting on top of the taxi that they had waiting for them. Their admirers sang the actresses' own songs to them and even accompanied them during their ride home.[104]

Food

• Amelie, the daughter of Lars Gronholt, sometimes did not eat her lunch, so he began to draw cartoons featuring superheroes who encouraged her to eat her lunch. In one cartoon, Thor bites into a sandwich, raises it high in the air, and says, "This sandwich—I like it!

Another!" In a comment on a story about Amelie and Lars, a woman who posts online using the name Napsauce wrote, "When I was in first grade, my dad drew on my lunch bags. Every single day, I got a new, full-color installment of 'The Adventures of Lunchman in Lunchland,' along with Lunchman's trusty sidekick, Alphonse the Armadillo. After lunch, I would carefully cut the illustration off the bag and paste it into a book. At the end of the school year I surprised him with the book of all his illustrations ... and 34 years later, he still has it, yellowed, faded, and a little crumbly, but still incredible. I was a lucky, lucky little girl." And GiantRubberGorilla wrote, "I used to take oranges and with my fingernail carve out two eyes and a smile—then I'd hand it to the kid and say—'Here. Tear off his face.' She loved it." And BigDaddy-O wrote, "I do a funny joke every day in my grade schooler's lunchbox. Something like: Q: Why did the rubber chicken cross the road? A: She wanted to stretch her legs. Then I say Love, Papa! I missed one day of doing this, and she was really put out! ;}"[105]

• Ballerina Illaria Obidenna Ladré lived through interesting times. When the *Titanic* struck an iceberg in 1912, she saw a huge sign on the main street in Petrograd: "*Titanic* Sunk." She also witnessed the Russian Tsar giving a watch to retiring actor Korgen Krukovskoy on 18 February 1917. It was the last watch the Tsar ever awarded because that night the Russian Revolution started. As Illaria left the theater with her mother, they heard shooting. Life during the Revolution was difficult. Illaria's sister got tuberculosis, so their mother bought a goat for its milk. Because they lived in a third-floor apartment, they arranged for another family to take care of the goat. Unfortunately, within three days the goat had disappeared—the other family had eaten it! Illaria and her family survived the Revolution, but at times the only food they had to eat was American kidney beans and Crisco. Sometimes, to get fuel to cook with, they were forced to tear up the parquet flooring from their apartment and burn it in a tin oven.[106]

• Reb Levi Yitzhak had a knack for looking on the bright side of things. Once he found a Jew eating during Tisha B'Av, the fast day set aside to remember the destruction of the Temple. Reb Yitzhak asked, "I suppose that you forgot that today is Tisha B'Av?" The Jew replied that he knew what day it was. Reb Yitzhak next asked, "I suppose you forgot that today is a fast day?" The Jew replied that he had not forgotten it. Reb Yitzhak then asked, "I suppose that you are ill and your physician has ordered you to eat on this fast day?" The Jew replied that he was in perfect health. Reb Yitzhak then prayed, "Lord of the Universe, see what a remarkable people Israel is! An Israelite will rather admit that he is a sinner than tell a lie!"[107]

• When George Balanchine took his New York City Ballet on tour to his native Russia, he was displeased with the behavior of his dancers, who engaged in a food fight in a Russian dining room because they found the food unappetizing. Mr. Balanchine chewed out his dancers, telling them that they were ambassadors from the United States to Russia and such behavior was unacceptable. Suzanne Farrell once mentioned to him that she liked the omelets, and trying to be helpful, Mr. Balanchine arranged with the Russian cooks to feed her omelets for breakfast, lunch, and supper. She ate hundreds of eggs during the tour.[108]

• An admirer of the young Margot Fonteyn invited her to dinner. She ordered the same thing he did—a sole *meunière*. Unfortunately, she had not eaten this dish before and soon found her mouth filled with bones. Her date ended up teaching her the finer points of eating fish. By the way, while in China, Ms. Fonteyn's father became a member of the Shanghai Club, where he was given advice about how to ward off illness in a foreign climate: "If you just remember always to keep about two inches of whiskey in the bottom of your stomach you will never have any trouble." He spent 20 years in China, and was never ill.[109]

• Clarinet player Irving Fazola liked hamburgers. Before a concert, he ate so many hamburgers that he got stuck—really stuck—in a chair and could not get up. Al Rose had hired him for the concert and wanted to play, so he used an ambulance and some strong men to carry Mr. Fazola and the chair to the concert stage. During intermission, Mr. Fazola was finally able to get out of the chair with the help of some strong men. He was even able to stand for his solos. After the concert, Mr. Fazola went to a restaurant—and ordered hamburgers.[110]

• While opera singer Mary Garden was sailing on the *Alfonso XIII*, she walked by—and smelled—the ship's kitchen, and she resolved never to eat anything that came out of that kitchen. Fortunately, she had some baskets of fruit that friends had given her as going-away gifts, and she lived off those. Whenever there was stormy weather, the fruit would tumble out of the baskets and bounce around the room. Ms. Garden amused herself by watching to see which fruit made it around the room first—it was always the pineapple.[111]

• Strange things happen in society. Glyndebourne was John Christie's ancient manor house in England. Once, his butler, Childs, interrupted a breakfast with bad news: "I'm sorry to disturb you, sir, but the cook's dead." One of the guests, a general, spoke up: "Under the circumstances, do you think I could get another sausage?" By the way, an American once asked Mr. Christie how he had gotten the Glyndebourne lawn to be so perfect. Mr. Christie replied, "It's easy—just mow it for 200 years."[112]

• Feodor Chaliapin sometimes clowned around on stage. During a performance of *Mefistofele* in Columbus, Ohio, he made co-star Claudia Muzio break out laughing by singing in Italian in front of the footlights, "Are we going to get a good spaghetti after the performance tonight?" By the way, while in America, mid-1950s Metropolitan Opera basso Cesare Siepi ate American food for a good reason: "In Memphis, how can I trust a plate of spaghetti? I have broiled meat and a salad."[113]

• Kirsten Flagstad was modest. Hearing that a flower had been named after her, she protested, "But you can't do that! It wouldn't be sensible! In my country, they name flowers only after important people!" By the way, Heinrich Conried's love of rich food did affect his life negatively in one way. He kept a box of bicarbonate of soda near him, and occasionally after dinner, he would reach for the box and say, "This is my lifesaver!"[114]

• Professional musicians are often asked to entertain at the dinners they attend. A wealthy society woman asked Fritz Kreisler to come to her dinner and to bring his violin, but he replied, "My violin never dines out." By the way, French composer Jules-Émile-Frédéric Massenet refused to have an Opus 13. His works are listed as Opus 12, Opus 12b, Opus 14.[115]

• Russian baritone Feodor Chaliapin sometimes grew weary of hostesses who invited him to dinner, then pressured him to sing for the other guests. He told one such hostess, "If you ask me to dinner, you feed me. If you ask me to sing, you pay me."[116]

• Harvard Law School professor Alan M. Dershowitz started a kosher deli named Maven's in 1988. On the menu appeared the slogan "Famous Since 5748"—in the Hebrew calendar, "5748" is equivalent to our calendar's "1988."[117]

• In Rialto, California, choreographer Twyla Tharp's parents built a drive-in theater, where she ate many dinners of such courses as candy corn, popcorn, ice cream bonbons, and Coke syrup.[118]

• Ballerina Natalia Makarova says that impresario Sol Hurok was a "devoted gourmet." Mr. Hurok once took her out to eat at a restaurant in Connecticut—the dinner lasted for five hours.[119]

Friends

• Penn Gillette of Penn and Teller fame respects thought. Once, he was taking a now-former girlfriend out to eat, but he needed to get some writing done first. It would take about an hour, and after apologizing to her, he said, "You can turn on the TV; my iPod has music on it and there are headphones right there. If you want to go out, my car keys are right there and there's a Starbucks in the lobby. I have a couple books there if you want to read and there's a magazine or two ...." But she said to him, "I'm fine. I'll just sit here." Penn asked her, "What are you going to do?" She replied, "I'll sit and think." In his book *God, No!*, Penn writes, "She's still one of my best friends and an inspiration."[120]

• A college professor once got upset because his students were only half-listening to his lecture, and he told them, "I'm offering you a dollar and you're taking only fifty cents." A friend of author Peg Bracken was in that course, and she says now that she didn't take even a nickel, for she can't remember the name of the course. By the way, Ms. Bracken has a friend who enjoys going to sleep, so he does it twice each night. He sets his alarm for 2 a.m., so that when it rings, he can shut it off and go back to sleep.[121]

• Robert Benchley met Donald Ogden Stewart on a rainy night as they were both coming out of a restaurant. Mr. Stewart saw a passerby with a large umbrella, pretended the passerby was a taxi, and took his arm and said, "Yale Club, please." Mr. Benchley then took Mr. Stewart's arm and said, "Can you drop me off at my place? It's on the way."[122]

Good Deeds

• On 5 November 2012 in Southfield Township, Michigan, Ty Houston, age 48, a home care registered nurse, was filling out his absentee ballot when a medical emergency occurred. He said, "I was filling out the form as were an elderly couple sitting at a nearby table. His wife, who was helping him fill out the ballot, asked him a couple of questions but he didn't respond. She screamed for help, and I went over to see what I could do." Mr. Houston laid the elderly man, who had a tracheotomy, on the floor and gave him emergency medical assistance. Mr. Houston said, "He was dead. He had no heartbeat and he wasn't breathing. I started CPR, and after a few minutes, he revived and started breathing again. He knew his name and his wife's name." Then he said something that showed what was important to him. Mr. Houston said, "The first question he asked was 'Did I vote?'" His wife said, "Your life is my concern." The elderly man told his wife that two things were important to him: "That I love you and that I finished what I came here to do: vote." He did vote, and he was taken to William Beaumont Hospital in Royal Oak, Michigan, after he had thanked Mr. Houston, who said, "It was God's divine word that I be there. Originally, I was just going to skip the ballot and just go to lunch that day." Clerk Sharon Tischler said, "It was definitely a 911 scenario. It was great there was someone around to render aid."[123]

• On Sunday, 25 January 1931, two days after Anna Pavlova (1881-1931) had died after a brief illness while on tour, a spotlight lit an empty stage—the Apollo Theater in London—and moved around as if seeking the missing ballerina while the orchestra played "The Dying Swan" in her memory. By the way, Ms. Pavlova supported her mother with a liberal allowance in her native Russia, but occasionally the Soviet government returned the money to her, saying that it would not tolerate "bourgeois charity."[124]

Husbands and Wives

• Artists Otto and Gertrud Natzler, a husband-and-wife team, worked in ceramics, and they lived in a part of California in which earthquakes were frequent—living there was not a good idea. During one earthquake, the lights went out and they could hear crashes coming from a closet in which they had stored many of their ceramic pieces. Of course, falling ceramic pieces were making the crashes. Gertrud listened to the crashes, and then she said to her husband, "Here goes our life's work." Fortunately, only a few works of art of art were totally destroyed. Many were unscathed, and others could be repaired.[125]

• As an international celebrity, Plácido Domingo occasionally receives romantic letters from women who don't know how devoted he is to his wife and three sons. One letter suggested that he and the letter writer ride away on a white horse "just like Don José and Carmen in the second act. After reading the letter, Mr. Domingo commented,

"She has conveniently forgotten what happens to Carmen in the fourth act!"[126]

Language

• Businesspeople need to take into account different cultures. Comic singer Anna Russell had an American agent, Eastman Boomer, but she toured frequently in England, necessitating that letters be written back and forth between Boomer and an English business manager. Boomer used to complain, "I don't know what the hell he's talking about. He writes two pages about the weather, the London scene, and enquires after my health, and he mentions business in the last paragraph as though it were an afterthought." Meanwhile, the Englishmen complained about Boomer's letters, "What's the matter with Boomer? He writes when he wants the tour, how much, yours faithfully. Hasn't he got any manners?" Ms. Russell was able to convince the Englishman to write more about business in his letters to Boomer, and she got Boomer to throw in some non-business paragraphs in his letters to the Englishmen, with the result that the two men ended up liking each other."[127]

• Léonide Massine found it difficult to learn English; however, he was happy when he learned that in England it is possible to get almost anything you want by using the word "please." By the way, Mr. Massine's name was originally "Miassin," but he changed it because Sergei Diaghilev felt that it was "too difficult" for audiences who spoke English. Also by the way, as a young man, Mr. Massine auditioned for Michel Fokine. Mr. Fokine asked him to study a mural on the wall, then imitate the poses of the characters on the mural. Mr. Massine did so, then Mr. Fokine asked him to jump over a chair that was three feet high to demonstrate his elevation. Mr. Massine did so easily—and passed the audition.[128]

• Michael Stephenson and Diane Downes were dancing the Snow *pas de deux* from *The Nutcracker*. During several rehearsals, Mr. Stephenson had forgotten a certain step, so when they arrived at that step, Ms. Downes, trying to be helpful, whispered, *"Effacé."* Unfortunately, Mr. Stephenson misheard the word and thought she was saying, "I feel sick," so trying to be helpful, he whispered encouraging words such as "You're doing fine" and "Hang in there." After the dance was over and they were safely offstage, Ms. Downes asked him, "What the hell were you talking about?"[129]

• Emmy Destinn was an opera singer from Czechoslovakia. During World War I, she suffered horribly while being interned in Austria, and after that experience, she vowed that never again would she speak German and she immediately dropped German operas from her repertoire. By the way, if you are in opera, you will mingle with many people from other countries, some of whom may not know English very well. Soprano Frances Alda was once toasted by her colleague De Segurola, who began by saying, "Alda, you permit? I speak on your behind ...."[130]

• Thomas Beecham once conducted in a building in Lancaster, England, in which this sign was hung: "It is strictly forbidden to use in this building the words Hell, Damn, and other Biblical Expressions." By the way, a sundial near Venice bears this Latin inscription: *Horas non numero nisi serenas.* (I count only the hours that are serene.) In other words, it counts only the hours that are sunny and pleasant.[131]

• Sir Steven Runciman, a British historian, told ballerina Margot Fonteyn about a parrot that had been named a professor. An old lady who was one of the very few people left who could speak Cornish owned the parrot. After the old lady died, only the parrot was able to speak Cornish, so London University gave the parrot its Chair of Cornish Language.[132]

• While in Germany, Percy Frosdick, a violinist with the London Philharmonic Orchestra, tried to remain on his vegetarian diet. When a waiter tried to serve him a steak, Mr. Frosdick declined it, saying, *"Nein, nein—ich bin Gemüse!"* Unfortunately, that means, "No, no—I am a vegetable!"[133]

• Irish playwright Brendan Behan often used the word "bejaysus" in conversation, causing many people to think he was being blasphemous. A man once asked Mr. Behan's friend Liam Dwyer about this practice, and Mr. Dwyer replied, "It's His friends who know Him by His first name."[134]

Media

• Fern Helsher worked as a press agent for Ted Shawn and His Men Dancers. As a former newspaper woman, she had many contacts and was able to get Mr. Shawn more and better publicity. Once, she went into the newspaper of a major midwestern city with publicity material, and the editor, who was a friend of hers, took her to lunch, where he asked, "What the hell are you representing a bunch of faeries for?" She replied, "They're not faeries, but let's not talk about them." She and the editor gossiped over lunch, and when she left, she gave the editor a package of photos, saying, "If you can do anything with it, fine. If not, OK." The next day photos of Ted Shawn and His Men Dancers were splashed all over the front page.[135]

• Alexander Woolcott used to tell this story: A city editor once sent a reporter to interview a man, but the man refused to be interviewed and threatened to shoot any reporter who rang his doorbell again. The alarmed reporter called his editor with this news, but the editor gave him this order, "You go back and tell that fellow he can't intimidate *me*."[136]

Mishaps

• Believe it or not, ballet has its intrigues. When Alicia Markova was about to dance the title role of *Giselle* in New York, someone in a crowd slipped this note into her hand: "DON'T DANCE TOMORROW NIGHT, OR...." In addition, the irate father of a ballerina who wanted to dance the role of Giselle on opening night punched Artistic Director Leonide Massine in the jaw. Despite the threats, Ms. Markova delivered a popularly and critically acclaimed performance that made her name in the United States. By the way, on one occasion, Ms. Markova, while dancing in the role of Giselle, started to pull some lilies from the stage, only to discover that the stagehands had mistakenly nailed them down. With a mighty effort, she wrenched them free, then continued to dance.[137]

• Gertrude Lawrence scored a notable success in Noel Coward's play *Private Lives*. After reading it, she definitely wanted to be a part of it, although it meant getting out of a contract to free herself to appear in it. Therefore, she sent Mr. Coward a telegram saying, "PLAY DELIGHTFUL STOP NOTHING WRONG THAT CANT BE FIXED." Unfortunately, Mr. Coward thought that "nothing wrong that can't be fixed" referred to his play, not to Ms. Lawrence's need to get out of a current contract, so he wired back that the only thing that needed to be fixed was Ms. Lawrence's acting. Fortunately, they got the misunderstanding straightened out, and *Private Lives* turned to be a major success for both of them.[138]

• Enrico Caruso enjoyed the absurdities that sometimes occur on the operatic stage. For example, in *Pagliacci*, the donkey that is brought onstage is very likely to upset the performance by misbehaving in some way. Such antics did not bother Mr. Caruso. He even occasionally announced, "I said a special prayer tonight that the donkey would behave bad. Then the people can laugh." By the way, Lucrezia Bori lost her voice, retired from opera, and returned to her native Spain. She regained her voice in a very unusual way. While she was riding on a mule, the mule became skittish and threw her from its back. After recovering from the fall, she found that her voice had returned in all its former glory, and so she returned to her operatic career.[139]

• People laughed at the opening of Giuseppe Verdi's *La Traviata*. One problem was that Fanny Salvini-Donatelli, a fat woman, played the part of a courtesan with tuberculosis. Whenever fat Fanny complained of wasting away, the audience roared with laughter. By the way, an 1855 American production of Mr. Verdi's *Ernani* was a disaster. In the finale, the tenor was supposed to stab himself with his sword, but when he drew it the blade went flying off, forcing the tenor to stab himself with the hilt. The tenor pretended to die, but he was too far forward on the stage, so that the curtain fell behind him, and the audience saw the "dead" man sit up, look around, then flee offstage.[140]

• When Jerome K. Jerome (1859-1927) was a young man acting in London, a play he was in was supposed to end spectacularly with a house falling on and killing the villain, while the hero rescued the heroine just in time. Fortunately, the house fell exactly as it was supposed to, the villain was killed exactly as he was supposed to be, and the hero rescued the heroine exactly as he was supposed to. Unfortunately, the curtain had fallen too quickly, and the audience saw none of the spectacle. Afterward, the manager spent considerable time looking for the man who had dropped the curtain too quickly. Perhaps it's just as well that the miscreant had run away, since the manager had a crowbar in his hands.[141]

• Trinette Singleton was performing with the Joffrey Ballet at the City Center in New York, when strange things started happening. First, she and the other dancers heard exclamations such as "Stop that!" and "Cut it out!" Then the music the orchestra was playing grew softer and softer and finally ceased. After exiting the stage, the dancers discovered what had happened. Some boys in the balcony had been throwing pieces of hard candy at the musicians, who had shouted at them to stop. The boys did not stop, so the musicians one by one had stopped playing and left the orchestra pit. Eventually, there was silence because conductor Allan Lewis had no musicians left to conduct.[142]

• African-American jazz great Duke Ellington once sleepily stumbled out of his sleeping car at a train station during a tour, then he joined a line of men climbing aboard a bus. The men turned out to be criminals, and the bus was taking them to prison. Fortunately, his road manager saw what had happened and chased down the bus with his car. It took a while, but eventually he managed to convince the driver that

Mr. Ellington was not a criminal, but a respected music composer and conductor.[143]

• Around 1914, while performing in New Orleans, Ma Rainey sang, "If you don't believe I'm sinkin', look what a hole I'm in." At that moment, the stage she was standing on collapsed. (Fortunately, no one was hurt.) In 1935, after touring and recording for decades as a professional singer, Ma Rainey retired and lived in Columbus, Georgia. On 22 December 1939, she died. The coroner listed the great blues singer's occupation as "Housekeeper."[144]

• At times, costumes create problems on stage. Ballet dancer Anthony Dowell was once dancing with Antoinette Sibley when the hook of his costume caught on her tutu. They had to run offstage to get unhooked. While he was dancing with Natalia Makarova, the same thing happened. Afterward, the stage manager said that he was tempted to pour a bucket of water over them because they looked like two dogs in heat.[145]

• Actress Maud Gill once wore a large picture hat on stage. Before one performance, a mouse got into the hat, and Ms. Maud put on the hat and unknowingly carried the mouse with her on stage, where the mouse's desperate attempts to escape entangled it in her hair. She was forced to take off the hat on stage, and the audience gasped at her taste in hairstyles.[146]

Chapter 4: From Money to Pride

Money

• When Fred Smith was an undergraduate at Yale University, he wrote a paper for an economics class that proposed the overnight delivery service that became FedEx. The overnight delivery service would have its own planes, depots, posting stations, and delivery vans. His professor gave him a C and wrote, "The concept is interesting and well-formed, but in order to earn better than a 'C,' the idea must be feasible." Mr. Smith started the company anyway, and like many or most beginning companies, it ran into financial difficulties. At one point, FedEx had only $5,000 in its checking account, and it had to pay a $24,000 jet fuel bill. Mr. Smith took the $5,000, flew to Las Vegas, played blackjack, and won $27,000. In 2012, FedEx was worth approximately $28 billion and Mr. Smith was worth approximately $2 billion.[147]

• A maggid (a traveling teacher-preacher) spread the word that in the World-to-Come, those who are wealthy in this World will be poor, and those who are poor in this World will be rich. Hearing this, a poor man asked the preacher for a loan so he could start a business in this World, saying that since he would be rich in the World-to-Come, he would repay the maggid there. The maggid listened, smiled, then pointed out a flaw in the poor man's logic: If the maggid lent the poor man money in this World to start a business and the business prospered, then he would be rich in this World, and therefore poor in the World-to-Come. How then could the man repay his debt to the maggid?[148]

• Operatic tenor Leo Slezak bought and fell in love with a 200-year-old peasants' cottage, which he had remodeled. At first, the architect tried to convince Mr. Slezak to tear down the peasants' cottage and build a new house, but after the cottage was remodeled, the architect admitted that he had been wrong because it really did make a beautiful house. Still, the architect wrote in Mr. Slezak's visitors' book, "When a fellow's got money, but the brains of a louse, / He'll buy an old ruin to make it a house."[149]

• Some opera fans are impoverished. In New York, a group of fans desperately wanted to hear Adelina Patti (1843-1919) sing in *La Traviata*, so they purchased the maximum number of tickets they could afford: one. Each fan watched 20 minutes of the performance—the first used the ticket as he entered, then got a "pass-out check" as he left the theater and handed it to the next fan. To keep everyone honest, the fans agreed that whoever stayed longer than 20 minutes would have to pay for the entire ticket.[150]

• Max D. Stein, a lawyer, liked to tell this story: A man came to see him about a legal question. A dog had come into his butcher shop and had run away with a $4 steak. His question was this: Is the dog's owner responsible for the loss of the steak? Mr. Stein replied that yes, the dog's owner is responsible. Hearing that, the man said, "Please pay the $4—it was your dog." Mr. Stein paid the $4, then said, "My minimum fee for legal advice is $500."[151]

• Being a ballet impresario is not necessarily (or likely!) a remunerative position. When Léonide Massine was choreographing ballets for Sergei Diaghilev, he was surprised to see that Mr. Diaghilev had holes in the soles of his shoes. And here is a bit of history trivia: Among the people who wrote to Serge Diaghilev saying they wished to become a member of his Ballets-Russes was the spy Mata Hari.[152]

• Jazz singer Anita O'Day was named Anita Belle Colton when she was born. She took the name O'Day because in pig Latin it means "dough," and she hoped to make a lot of dough as a professional walkathon contestant. (During the Depression, people tried to make money winning marathon walks, where they walked for days in front of an audience with only occasional 15-minute breaks.)[153]

• On Purim, many pious Jews distribute money to the poor. R' Avraham Yehoshua Heshel of Apta once counted money over and over again before Purim. His son saw him counting the money, and said, "Father, I thought you hate money." R' Avraham Yehoshua Heshel replied, "I want to distribute this money to the poor. If it means nothing to me, then my gift will be of no significance."[154]

• Theater director Tyrone Guthrie could be frugal at times. Once, he reserved tickets to see Paul Muni in *Inherit the Wind*. However, he arrived late, just after Act One. The ticket seller named the price for his ticket, but a somewhat inebriated Mr. Guthrie said, "That's for three acts; what's the price for two?"[155]

• Corey Ford's writings were widely plagiarized—especially his short humorous piece "How to Guess Your Age." Whenever this happened, Mr. Ford would sue, winning every case. He once said about his lawsuits, "I find this a much easier way to make a living than by writing."[156]

• Basso Karl Formes loved the performing arts so much that in his early, impoverished years he once swam a river to see an actor because he did not have enough money for both passage on the ferry boat and a ticket for the play.[157]

Music

• Dizzy Gillespie played a trumpet that had an unusual shape. Its bell did not point forward but up—at a 45-degree angle. He says, "The truth is that the shape of my horn is an accident. I could pretend that I went into the basement and thought it up, but it wasn't that way." So how did the shape come about? A man accidentally sat on it, and the bell bent. It was 6 January 1953, the birthday of Dizzy's wife, and he played at the party for her. He liked the sound of the unusually shaped trumpet. He says that "when the bell bent, it made a smaller hole because of the dent. I couldn't get the right sound, but it was a strange sound that I got from the instrument that night. I played it, and I liked the sound. The sound had been changed, and it could be played softly, very softly, not blarey." The next day he had the trumpet straightened, but it missed the sound that the trumpet had had. He contacted the Martin Company and had an artist draw a trumpet with a bell at a 45-degree angle and told them, "I want a horn like this." They told him, "You're crazy!" Dizzy said, "'OK, I'm crazy, but I want a horn like this.' They made me a trumpet, and I've been playing one like that ever since."[158]

• Some music trivia: 1) Q: Who wrote Henry Purcell's *Trumpet Voluntary*? A: Jeremiah Clarke (1670?-1707) composed the *Trumpet Voluntary*, but many people thought it was too good to have been written by him, so Henry Purcell (1659?-1695) was given the credit for composing it. 2) Johann Sebastian Bach (1685-1750) took organ music seriously. He once walked 200 miles to hear the great organist Dietrich Buxtehude. 3) It helps to have long fingers if you are a pianist or an organist so that you can more easily reach widely separated keys. According to music historian Charles Burney, Johann Sebastian Bach sometimes used a stick in his mouth to strike keys he couldn't reach with either hand. 4) George Frideric Handel (1685-1759) composed his *Water Music* for King George I of England. At its premiere, King George I sailed on a barge on the Thames, while another barge nearby played the *Water Music*. 5) Orlando di Lasso was a boy singer in Belgium in the 16th century. He was such a good singer that rival choirs kidnapped him three times.[159]

• A few music anecdotes: 1) Conductor Wilhelm Furtwängler once ordered the musicians of the London Philharmonic Orchestra not to cross their legs as he felt that it looked unprofessional. At the very next performance, without any planning, every member of the orchestra whose instrument permitted it had his or her legs crossed when Maestro Furtwängler came out to conduct. When he raised the baton, they all uncrossed their legs. Later, Maestro Furtwängler apologized to the orchestra. 2) Conductor Georg Solti once told singer John Lanigan, "John, dear, I beat it in twelve here." Mr. Lanigan replied, "Don't worry, Maestro. I never look." Sir Georg laughed. (Don't worry—this anecdote uses music jargon that doesn't need to be censored.) 3) Sir Malcolm Sargent once publicly rehearsed a piece written by Vaughan Williams, making alterations as he went along. Suddenly, a voice came from the audience, "Hey! What are you doing to my piece?" The voice belonged to Mr. Williams himself.[160]

• A few jazz music anecdotes: 1) Jazz musician Wynton Marsalis believes that it takes more skill to play jazz than it takes to play classical music. In 1984, he won Grammys for making both kinds of music—he won as Best Classical Soloist with Orchestra and as Best Jazz Soloist. He also decided that year to devote himself solely to playing jazz. 2) As a young boy, jazz musician Louis Armstrong frequently did not have enough food to eat. He sometimes scavenged through garbage cans looking for something edible. 3) Some musicians played for Duke Ellington for most of their careers. For example, Harry Carney joined Mr. Ellington's band in 1927 when he was 17 years old and was still playing for him 47 years later, when Mr. Ellington died. 4) Charlie "Bird" Parker was a genius while playing the saxophone, but far from a genius while attending school. He once said that he had "spent three years in high school and wound up a freshman."[161]

• Famous violinist Eduard Reményi used to amaze audiences by seeming to play a long low note at the same time he played a series of high notes. Such a feat is impossible, and this is the trick he used: While he stood on stage playing the series of high notes, backstage an organist played the long low note. By the way, Niccolo Paganini was such a gifted violinist that after hearing him play, a professional musician by the name of Mori raised his own violin over his head and offered to sell it for only eighteen cents. Also by the way, famous violinist August Wilhemj knew how to make a violin sound good and how to make it sound bad. When he wanted to sell a violin, he played it and made it sound good, and when he wished to buy a violin, he played it and made it sound bad.[162]

• At Oxford, the organist of Magdalen was John Varley Roberts, a choral trainer who was outspoken when it came to voice theory. After a convention in which many papers on the training of voices were read, Mr. Roberts called together his choir and told them, "Now, lads, you have heard a great deal about the voice in the last few days, but I've got just this to say to you and don't you forget it. All you've got to do is to stand up, throw your heads back and sing; all the rest's humbug." By the way, when Richard Strauss wanted more volume from his orchestra in his opera *Salome*, he encouraged the musicians to greater efforts by telling them that the singers could still be heard.[163]

• Outlaw country music singer Willie Nelson tells this politically incorrect joke: A man saw his wife using an enlarging cream on her breasts, so he told her, "Don't use the cream. Use toilet paper—look what it's done to your butt." By the way, here are a couple of Willie Nelson quotes: 1) "Every song is a gospel song. All music is sacred. Every note of music in the world is spiritual and sacred ... and that's the gospel truth. Amen." 2) "God has blessed you richly, so get down on your knees and thank Him. Don't forget the less fortunate or God will personally kick your *ss. I'd love to do it for Him, but I can't be everywhere at once. Amen."[164]

• A conductor once tried to use poetic language to describe how some music should sound: "The music should sound as if you were playing on top of a high mountain, overlooking a bank of clouds. You are fanned by the winds ...." The concertmaster, however, thought that this was nonsense and said, "Look, just tell us whether you want the music played loud or soft." By the way, Walter Damrosch once conducted at a benefit concert that featured sixteen different pianists. Before he started conducting, he turned to the audience and joked, "What they need here is not a conductor, but a traffic cop."[165]

• Occasionally, Sir Thomas Beecham conducted music in which he had little interest. Viola virtuoso Lionel Tertis once speculated that Sir Thomas had given an entire program of "weak, sentimental French music" simply to prove that he could fill the concert hall no matter what program he conducted. Once, during a rehearsal of a piece of music in which Sir Thomas had no interest whatsoever, he continued to conduct after the piece had ended. When orchestra leader Albert Sammons whispered, "Sir Thomas, we have finished the work," Sir Thomas replied, "Thank God for that!"[166]

• In 1713, Giuseppe Tartini had a dream in a monastery where he was staying. In the dream, the Devil offered to buy Tartini's soul for whatever price he wanted. Mr. Tartini made request after request, all of which the Devil granted, then, being a composer, Mr. Tartini requested that the Devil provide him with a sonata. The devil played a beautiful sonata on a violin, and Mr. Tartini fainted. In the morning, he did his best to recreate the Devil's sonata, but felt as if he had recreated only part of it. Because of the inspiration he had received, Mr. Tartini called the sonata *The Devil's Trill*.[167]

• George Frideric Handel's father wanted him to be a lawyer, not a composer, so he was against his son's learning to play musical instruments. Fortunately, Handel's mother was sympathetic to his love of music, and she smuggled a clavichord into the attic for him to practice on while his father was asleep. By the way, after hearing Mr. Handel's *Messiah* in London, Thomas Hay, Lord Kinnoull, told the composer that *Messiah* is "a fine entertainment." Handel replied, "I should be sorry if I only entertained them. I wish to make them better."[168]

• Fritz Kreisler was playing his violin before the Sultan and his Court in Turkey when the Sultan began to clap his hands. Feeling immensely flattered, Mr. Kreisler played on, and the more he played, the harder the Sultan clapped his hands. Finally, the Grand Vizier said urgently to Mr. Kreisler, "Do you wish to lose your head? Don't you hear His Majesty clapping his hands?" Mr. Kreisler replied that indeed he had heard the clapping, but what of it? The Grand Vizier exclaimed, "What of it? Why, the Sultan is giving you the signal to stop!"[169]

• Famous pianist Moritz Rosenthal had a sharp tongue. While visiting the home of a Viennese composer (not named), he saw several scores by such notabilities as Bach, Beethoven, and Mozart. Mr. Rosenthal exclaimed, "My goodness! I always thought you composed by ear." By the way, after listening to a premiere of a work by Johannes Brahms, a Viennese composer said, "A splendid work, your new symphony, only sometimes it reminds me of some other music." Insulted, Mr. Brahms snapped, "What other music—your next symphony?"[170]

• Oscar Levant studied piano for several years under Sigismund Stojowski. Once Mr. Stojowski asked him what he was going to play for a certain program. Mr. Levant replied, I think I'll play Debussy's '*Reflets dans L'Eau*' or '*Poissons d'Or*.'" Mr. Stojowski then said, "Your piano playing is not improving, but your French is." By the way, Mr. Levant and George Gershwin were friends for many years. In fact, a chapter in Mr. Levant's book *A Smattering of Ignorance* is titled "My Life, or the Story of George Gershwin."[171]

• Gioacchino Rossini's mother wondered how one of his operas had been received. He sent her a drawing of an Italian straw-covered bottle—the kind called "fiasco." By the way, when Mr. Rossini was 70 years old, his friends collected 20,000 francs so they could make a statue of Mr. Rossini and put it on a pedestal. Mr. Rossini joked that he would stand on the pedestal if his friends would give him the money.[172]

• In 1929, Yehudi Menhuin made his debut at Carnegie Hall, where he played the violin brilliantly. In the audience were Mischa Elman, who was a violinist like Mr. Menhuin, and Alexander Brailowsky, a pianist. As Mr. Menhuin awed the audience with his virtuoso performance, Mr. Elman turned to Mr. Brailowsky and said, "Don't you think it's hot in here?" Mr. Brailowsky replied, "Not for pianists."[173]

• Early in his career, American dance pioneer Ted Shawn toured with a show that used local musicians to provide accompaniment for the dances. At one town, the local trombone player was so bad that the conductor pointed to him, then said, "Out!" The trombone player replied, "I'm mayor of this town. Either I play or there won't be any show."[174]

• Writer Charles MacArthur once attended a party given by music critic Samuel Chotzinoff, who invited many of the world's best classical musicians and asked them to perform. Mr. Chotzinoff became angry because many of his guests preferred to listen to Mr. MacArthur tell anecdotes in the kitchen instead of listening to the classical music.[175]

• Hans von Bülow once made a notable joke and criticism when he appeared as pianist after a woman vocalist had poorly sung a solo. He sat down at the piano and warmed up by playing a passage from the finale of Beethoven's Ninth Symphony—the entrance of the baritone singing, "O brothers, no longer these sad tones!"[176]

• Addison Mizner once snuck away from a musical entertainment at a party in order to play pinochle with his host in another room. His hostess, Mrs. E.T. Stotesbury, tracked him down and complained, "You sneak away when Rachmaninoff is playing!" Mr. Mizner replied, "I thought it was the piano tuner."[177]

• Ben Dorcy, a band boy who has worked with some of the most famous celebrities in country music, once was asked, "How do you get started in this business?" He replied, "There ain't but one way. You start at the bottom and go right to the top. Don't mess with that in-between sh*t."[178]

• Opera singer Enrico Caruso's brother, Giovanni, once became so angry at their mother that he removed a straw hat she was wearing and bit a piece out of its brim.[179]

Opera

• Colonel James H. Mapleson (1830-1901) once had to change the bill of an opera performance seven times in New York before he could find an opera that was playable. Originally, he had scheduled *William Tell*, but he had to cancel that because his prima donna fell ill. Next, he scheduled *Lucia di Lammermoor*; unfortunately, soprano

Laura Zagury then informed him that she had never sung the role Colonel Mapleson wanted her to sing. Therefore, he changed the opera to *Aida*—but was informed that another prima donna had fallen ill. He then decided to schedule *Rigoletto*, but one of his principal singers told him that she was not prepared to sing her part. Next, Colonel Mapleson scheduled *Les Huguenots*, but discovered that one of his singers, believing that she would not called upon to sing that night, had taken some medicine that rendered her unable to perform. Colonel Mapleson then scheduled *La Favorita*, which was performed.[180]

• Marietta Alboni (1823-1894), a contralto, once heard of a plot by some Italian patriots to have her hissed off the opera stage simply because she had been singing in foreign countries to foreigners. She learned that the conspirators were meeting at a certain tavern, so she put on men's clothing, went to the tavern, and while pretending to be a man, joined the conspirators. They gave the new conspirator a whistle and said that it should be blown at a certain point in the performance, which would signal to everyone that the hissing should begin. After Ms. Alboni made her entrance on stage that night, wearing the whistle on a chain around her neck, a couple of conspirators began to hiss without waiting for the signal. Ms. Alboni walked to the front of the stage, held up the whistle, then said, "Gentlemen, are you not a little before your time?" Recognizing that they had been tricked, but being good sports, the conspirators gave her an ovation.[181]

• The Teatro la Fenice in Venice, Italy, is the only opera house in the world that has an entrance for gondolas. (The theater is built oddly because the site it is on is shaped irregularly, partly due to the presence of canals.) It was built in 1836 to replace another theater that had burned down. Gianantonio Selva, who designed the building, had the word "*Societas*" written on the building's facade. Witty Venetians made an acrostic of the word: "*Sine Ordine Cum Irregularitate Erexit Theatrum Antonius Selva.*" Translated, the phrase means: "Without

Order, With Irregularity, This Theater was Built by Antonio Selva."[182]

• In 1951, Eugene Conley, a tenor for the Metropolitan Opera, bought a homestead with no water or heating or other modern conveniences in New Jersey. A stream called Plum Brook ran through the 50-acre property, suggesting a name for the estate: Plumbroke Farm. By the way, mid-1950s Metropolitan Opera baritone Frank Guarrera grew up in Philadelphia with parents who had emigrated from Italy. His parents continued their wine-making in Philadelphia, and little Frank sometimes went to school with his hands stained red from the grapes used for wine.[183]

• African-American diva Martina Arroyo remembers some very under-rehearsed performances in Europe. Once, in Frankfurt, Germany, she walked onto the stage in the role of Aida without knowing which singer on stage was playing Aida's father—until the baritone playing the father started singing. By the way, during a rehearsal of *Un Ballo in Maschera*, Ms. Arroyo walked out on stage—wearing a fake beard.[184]

Parents

• In the early 1930s, for Norma Jeane's sixth birthday, her mother, Gladys Mortensen, arranged a special surprise. As Norma Jeane watched, an airplane circled her house and the pilot waved to her. Unfortunately, Norma Jeane's mother was unable to take care of her, putting her in a foster home when she was 12 days old, but visiting whenever she could. Later, Norma Jeane's mother developed mental illness and spent much of the rest of her life in mental institutions. Norma Jeane was raised in a succession of foster homes, homes of some relatives and friends, and even an orphanage. Despite her difficult early life, Norma Jeane became famous as movie star Marilyn Monroe. By the way, in 1962, Ms. Monroe sang "Happy Birthday" to President John F. Kennedy in a breathless, sexy voice. Afterward, President Kennedy said,

"Thank you. I can now retire from politics after having had 'Happy Birthday' sung to me in such a sweet, wholesome way."[185]

• In 1952, Walt Disney took his wife and two young daughters to Europe, with first a stopover in New York. His daughters wanted to go for a short visit to Washington D.C., and Walt told them, "If you want to go, then go ahead." Such a trip—alone—would be a first for them. They asked him what they should do. He told them, "You're old enough to think for yourselves. Go down and ask the porter; he'll tell you about trains." They left to seek information from the porter. Mrs. Disney explained to a reporter what Walt did next: "The minute they left the room, he called the porter and told him exactly what he wanted done. Then he called the hotel in Washington and gave explicit instructions. The girls had a whirl for themselves, of course, and they'll never know until they read this that their father arranged the whole thing."[186]

• Penn Jillette of Penn and Teller fame uses profanity a lot, but he did not use profanity around his mother and father because it would have made them uncomfortable. His mother read the *Playboy* and *Rolling Stone* interviews with him and said, "It's amazing how they have to add all that swearing to how you talk to make it fit in their magazine." He explained to her that he really does talk that way, but that he did not use profanity around her and around his father. She shrugged, and Penn is not sure that she believed him.[187]

Pranks

• Danish tenor Lauritz Melchior enjoyed playing practical jokes. At a performance of *Gotterdammerung*, Frida Leider, playing Brunnhilde, approached the corpse of Siegfried, expecting to find Mr. Melchior lying there. Instead, she found a stranger—and she saw Mr. Melchior merrily waving to her from the wings. By the way, after a bad experience early in his career, Italian tenor Beniamino Gigli wanted to be paid in cash before each performance. He used to put the money in his back pocket, so in between arias he could pat it. By the way, Mr. Gigli knew that English speakers found it difficult to pronounce his name correctly, so he told them to call him "Mr. Giggly." Also by the way, as a child, German soprano Elizabeth Schumann enjoyed the theater, and she used to sneak out of her house at night and walk to a nearby theatre to enjoy the performances of a traveling troupe.[188]

• In 1996, one of the student hacks (pranks) at MIT was the replacing of the "No Trespassing" signs at the entrance to the computer clusters with signs that stated, "You must be at least this smart to use Athena workstations," complete with a graph that charted levels of intelligence. The bottom intelligence level was "Urchins who log in as root." In the middle intelligence levels were "average Harvard student," "average B.U. [Boston University] student," and "average CalTech student." Holding the top intelligence level was "below-average MIT student." In the 1980s an elevator hacker replaced the word "UP" with "Heaven" and the word "DOWN" with "MIT."[189]

• Norwegian violinist Ole Bull once played a practical joke on the public. After playing a Norwegian melody as an encore piece, he held his bow over the strings of his violin long after the sound had ceased, then as he left the stage, he murmured to a friend, "Did I not play it finely on the public?" Sure enough, many members of the audience thought that Ole Bull was able to hear tones that were inaudible to most other people. And sure enough, some members of the audience thought that they had sensitive enough ears to hear the sound that Ole Bull had, they supposed, made and heard.[190]

• To film the *Gilligan's Island* episode titled "It's a Bird, It's a Plane, It's Gilligan," Bob Denver, who played Gilligan, was suspended by a cable 50 feet above the stage. Mr. Denver looked down and saw two crew members holding the cable suspending him above the stage. One of the crew members said to the other crew member, "Let's go get a cup of coffee," and then they let go of the cable and walked away. Mr. Denver screamed—but he hadn't fallen an inch. The cable was tied to the stage, and the two crew members had only pretended to be holding the cable.[191]

• In George Bernard Shaw's *St. Joan*, the Inquisitor has a 14-minute speech in the trial scene. In a mid-1960s production, Harold Innocent played the role of the Inquisitor. At a final run-through of the scene before the play opened, the cast pulled an elaborate practical joke. As Mr. Innocent began his 14-minute speech, the other cast members started drinking tea, knitting, playing cards, playing chess, and doing crosswords.[192]

• Once, in the middle of the night, a woman named Gisella Werbezirk-von Piffl was awakened by the ringing of her telephone. When she answered, a voice asked, "Is this Gisella Werbezirk-von Piffl?" When she said it was, the voice asked, "Did you by any chance go to school with me in New York City?" When she answered "No," the voice replied, "I'm sorry. I must have phoned the wrong Gisella Werbezirk-von Piffl."[193]

Pride

• Actress Beatrice Lillie once was in Chicago trying on dresses she had ordered made when Mrs. Swift, a member of a wealthy meat-packing family, also arrived to try on some dresses. Unaccustomed to being kept waiting, the wealthy, snobbish woman loudly sent her assistant to "tell that actress that she was delaying Mrs. Swift." Ms. Lillie, who happened to be married to Lord Peel of the British aristocracy, kept Mrs. Swift waiting a good while, then said loudly, so that she would be overheard by her, "Tell the butcher's wife that Lady Peel has finished now."[194]

• The Jewish movement known as Hasidism is very much opposed to pride. Once, an opponent of Hasidism complained to Rebbe Wolfe of Zhitomir, "My son has begun to study Hasidism, and he talks constantly about fighting his pride. I don't understand my son. He does nothing and he knows nothing, so what does he have to be proud about? Look at me. I have studied with famous teachers, I have memorized half the Torah, I give charity generously, and I attend religious services three times a day. Do I look like I need to fight pride?"[195]

Chapter 5: From Problem-Solving to Yom Kippur

Problem-Solving

• Leonard Reed was very light-skinned and blue-eyed—his father was white, and his mother was part black and part Choctaw Cherokee. In the United States, that meant that Mr. Reed was considered black. However, throughout his tap dancing career in the early part of the 20th century, he switched from performing as a white man to performing as a black man as opportunities for work arose. As a child, he entered and won a dance contest for whites, but someone told the manager of the theater that he was black, so he grabbed the prize money and ran. The manager yelled, "Catch that n*gger," but everyone looked around and asked, "Where?" Young Leonard blended in by also yelling, "Catch that n*gger," and so he was able to get away.[196]

• In July 1996, Boris Yeltsin was worried about getting enough votes to be reelected President of Russia. Many of his supporters lived in cities, and he was afraid that they would leave the cities and go to their country cottages and have a good time and not bother to vote. He wanted them to stay in the cities and vote for him. He found a way to do just that. *Tropikanka* was a very popular television soap opera in Russia. The soap opera broadcast three new episodes between 8 a.m. and 11 a.m. on election day. Most country cottages did not have televisions, so people stayed in the cities, watched the three episodes, and then had plenty of time left over to vote. Mr. Yeltsin won the election by more than 10 million votes.[197]

• This story from the Babylonian Talmud, Kiddushin 81a, shows how a rabbi prevented himself from engaging in unethical behavior. Some women stayed on an upstairs floor at the house of Rabbi Amram the Pious. As one of the women walked by, Rabbi Amram saw that she was beautiful, and he grabbed a ladder and set it up so he could go upstairs. But halfway up the ladder, he shouted, "A fire is burning in Rabbi Amram's house!" His disciples came, saw the rabbi halfway up the ladder, and knowing that he was filled with lust for one of the women upstairs, they told him, "You have made us put you to shame." Rabbi Amram replied, "Better that you shame Amram in this world than be ashamed of him in the next."[198]

• Like many star actors, William Charles Macready was accused of hogging the stage. He acted frequently with Helena Faucit, and *Punch* once stated that Mr. Macready must think that Ms. Faucit had a beautiful back, because that was all he allowed the audience to see of her. By the way, Mr. Charles Macready once contrived a bit of stage business in which he rumpled the hair of the character played by Ellen Terry. However, this annoyed Ms. Terry. She requested that he stop doing this, but he continued. Therefore, to solve the problem, she stuck several pins in her hair with the sharp ends pointing up.[199]

• To celebrate the reopening of the arena at Alexandra Palace, Sir Ralph Richardson was asked to perform a speech from Shakespeare on television. Sir Ralph thought for a moment, then he said, "I think I shall do my speech from *Richard IV* or *Henry X*—I know it by heart." Then he spoke several minutes of a speech that was complete rubbish but which sounded authentic. Sir Ralph then asked, "Shall I stop, or continue? That's the speech I used to do whenever I dried [forgot my lines] in Shakespeare, no critic ever noticed it, no audience has ever made any comment on it whatsoever."[200]

• The great dancer Bill Robinson, aka Mr. Bojangles, protected himself against interlopers. While performing at the Cotton Club, Mr. Bojangles noticed members of the Tramp Band talking during his dance act, so when the Tramp Band was on later, he got hold of a tin plate and beat it while wandering through the audience, calling, "Peanuts! Peanuts!" The audience was too busy laughing at Mr. Bojangles' antics to notice the Tramp Band. After that experience, members of the Tramp Band were respectful—and quiet—during Mr. Bojangles' performance.[201]

• Soprano Giuseppina Grassini once refused to sing at a performance in place of her arch-rival, Mrs. Elizabeth Billington, but fast-thinking stage manager Michael Kelly told her that the Queen had intended to attend the performance incognito and would be disappointed if the performance were cancelled. Ms. Grassini decided to do the performance. Later, she found out that she had been fooled and the Queen was not present, but by that time she was succeeding in her performance so well that she didn't mind being fooled.[202]

• Walt Disney stuck up for his employees. One of his employees mowed the grass by the window of a visiting film company executive who was so annoyed that he shouted at the employee. Mr. Disney called the executive into his office and told him, "You spoke harshly to that man. He's been with me for 20 years. I don't want it to happen again." The executive replied, "Yes, sir." By the way, Mr. Disney once stated what he felt was the way to success: "Quit talking—and start doing it."[203]

• Everett Greenbaum was a writer for *The Andy Griffith Show* and the man who created Gomer Pyle. Mr. Greenbaum had driven into a gasoline station with engine trouble, but the only thing the incompetent station attendant could think to do to fix the problem was to add more gasoline to the gas tank. The incompetent station attendant became the model for Gomer. By the way, here's a bit of TV trivia: On the television sitcom *M*A*S*H*, no laughtrack is used in the operating room scenes.[204]

• In vaudeville, theater owners had a problem with "stayovers"—people who would see the show and then stay over to see it again, thus reducing the number of tickets that could be sold for the next show. At the New York Paramount, the show used to close with a community "follow the bouncing ball" sing-along, which always ended with "The Star-Spangled Banner" to get people on their feet and inclined to walk out of the theater.[205]

• In the old days, ballet dancers seldom made much money. While performing with the Ballet Russe de Monte Carlo in the late 1930s, the younger dancers got accommodations by playing the "Army Game." One dancer would rent a room in a hotel, then six or seven other dancers would join that person. Together, they bribed a maid to bring them lots of towels. Without the Army Game, they would not have been able to stay in a hotel.[206]

• Wilson Mizner wanted good service. Once he went to a restaurant, but the servers were slow in getting him a pack of cigarettes he had asked for, so Mr. Mizner used a telephone to order that a District Telegraph Service messenger boy be sent to him. When the messenger boy arrived, Mr. Mizner sent him to get cigarettes from the restaurant's cigar stand, then gave him a very large tip. After that, he received excellent service in the restaurant.[207]

• Drama critic Robert Benchley was frequently annoyed by women at matinees, who talked during the play he had to review. Once, at the end of the first act, he told two noisy women sitting directly behind him, "I hope you'll excuse me, but if you two ladies would be so kind as to leave the theater, I shall be more than glad to pay for your seats." The two women were quiet for the rest of the play.[208]

Puns

• Composer Igor Stravinsky learned English late in life, but he learned it well. He enjoyed making puns in English, and while dining one evening, he asked for a dish of tongue by saying, "Please pass the language." By the way, at 4:30 a.m. one day ballerina Maria Tallchief woke up to find her then-husband, George Balanchine, missing. She got up, searched for him, and found him in the kitchen, cooking the Easter meal—something she learned he did each year.[209]

• Lord Kames was not known for prodigality in offering good wine to his guests, although he did serve a port of low quality. One day, his guest was the Hon. Henry Erskine. When the conversation turned to the fleet of Sir Charles Hardy, which the French were blockading, Erskine said, "They are, like us, confined to port."[210]

• During a rehearsal for *H.M.S. Pinafore*, Sir William Schwenck Gilbert told heavily built Rutland Barrington to sit on a skylight "pensively." Unfortunately, Mr. Barrington was too heavy for the skylight and it broke. "For goodness' sake, Barrington," Sir William complained. "I said 'pensively,' not 'expensively.'"[211]

• Lord Tinwald (1680-1763) once spoke to a man named Mr. Lamb, who confessed that although he was a lawyer and often spoke before the court, the act of public speaking still made him nervous. Lord Tinwald replied, "It's nothing unusual that a lamb should grow sheepish."[212]

Rabbis

• Some rabbis think that a white lie is permissible when telling it will avoid hurting someone's feelings. Why do they think this? When God told Abraham, who was 99 years old, that his wife, Sarah, would bear his child, Sarah was eavesdropping. She laughed to herself and said, "Now that I am withered, am I to have enjoyment, with my husband so old?" God then said to Abraham, "Why did Sarah laugh, saying, 'Shall I in truth bear a child, old as I am?'" Apparently, God did not want to hurt Abraham's feelings, or cause discord between man and wife, by relating what Sarah had said about his age.[213]

• A rabbi once went to a rich man on a cold winter night to ask for money to buy coal for poor people. The rich man came to the door, but the rabbi declined to go inside. Instead, the rabbi kept the rich man answering question after question about the health of his family as the rich man stood shivering in his doorway. Finally, the rabbi brought up the topic of charity for the poor. Because the rich man now understood how people suffer from the cold, he made a substantial donation.[214]

Sermons

• Two young rabbis were in competition to serve at a prominent synagogue. As part of the interview process, each rabbi was to give a sample sermon. One rabbi did not bother to write a sermon but instead took it easy and listened as the other rabbi practiced his sermon over and over again. The next day the lazy rabbi was invited to give his sermon first, so he stood up and recited the diligent rabbi's sermon, which he had learned by hearing it so often. Then the diligent rabbi was invited to give his sermon. The diligent rabbi was angry, of course, at the lazy rabbi for stealing his sermon, but since it was the only sermon he had prepared, he was forced to give this same sermon in the synagogue. The members of the committee for selecting a rabbi were astonished at this rabbi for repeating word for word the sermon the first rabbi had given, and they elected him their rabbi because anyone who can hear a sermon once and repeat it word for word must have a brilliant mind.[215]

• Scottish preachers can be outspoken. The Reverend Mr. Scott, of the Cowgate in Edinburgh, once told his congregation, "My brethren, Job, in the first place, was a sorely tried man. Job, in the second place, was an uncommonly patient man. Job, in the third place, never preached here at the Cowgate. Fourthly, and lastly, if Job had preached here, God help his patience." By the way, after hearing a sermon, a Scotswoman criticized it by saying it had three faults: "First, it was read. Second, it wasn't well read. And third, it wasn't worth reading." Also by the way, this verse can be found in Scotland's Elgin Cathedral: "If lyfe were a thing that monie could buy, / The poor could not live, and the rich would not die."[216]

• Here are two anecdotes about sermons: 1) A preacher led a service that was attended by a former Republican governor of the state of Indiana. In his sermon, the preacher told about the Pharisee and the publican, and he said, "But the Republican would not so much as lift his eyes up into heaven." 2) A pastor once spoke on the sin of adultery, and as he spoke, a balloon from a youth group party floated behind him—the balloon had a big smiley face.[217]

• The Maggid of Kelm repeated his sermons, giving the same few sermons over and over. Once, a sinner asked him, "Why do you keep repeating your sermons over and over?" The Maggid replied, "Why do you keep repeating your sins over and over?"[218]

Television

• In 2003, Juan Catalan, a 24-year-old machinist, was accused of murder. He protested that he had been attending a Los Angeles Dodgers game at Dodger Stadium at the time of the murder. He had the ticket stubs, but he needed more evidence to show that he was at the game. As it happened, the TV show *Curb Your Enthusiasm* had filmed an episode in Dodger Stadium on the day that Mr. Catalan had attended the game. The show was contacted, and a viewing of the footage shot that day showed Mr. Catalan and his daughter eating hot dogs in the stands. Mr. Catalan, who had spent five months in prison, escaped the death penalty. Larry David, the main man behind *Curb Your Enthusiasm*, says now, "I tell people that I've done one decent thing in my life, albeit inadvertently."[219]

• Lots of fans of *The Avengers* think that Mrs. Emma Peel and Mr. John Steed should have gotten romantically involved. In a way, they did. When Diana Rigg, who played Mrs. Peel, decided to leave the series, the writers brought back her supposedly dead husband, test pilot Peter Peel, by having him found alive in the Amazon jungle. In the episode "The Forget-Me-Knot," Mrs. Peel and Steed say goodbye (this is the only time Steed ever calls her "Emma") then she leaves with Peter Peel. However, Peter Peel was played by actor Patrick Macnee, who also played John Steed.[220]

• Aaron Ruben was the producer of *The Andy Griffith Show*, which featured Mr. Griffith as Sheriff Andy Taylor and Don Knotts as his incompetent deputy, Barney Fife. Once, someone told Mr. Knotts that Aaron Ruben thought there was a lot of Don Knotts in Barney Fife.

Mr. Knotts replied, "Gee, I hope not *too* much!" By the way, Mr. Griffith was a well-liked man. One of the writers for the series, Harvey Bullock, named his only son "Andy."[221]

• A 1990s TV commercial for a Norwegian life insurance company showed two men meeting, then taking off in a glider. Seconds after they are in the air, two more men arrive—they are the instructors for the first two men.[222]

Theater

• Actor-manager Sir Herbert Beerbohm Tree (1853-1917) was a perfectionist. During a rehearsal of a thunderstorm on stage, a real thunderstorm blew up outside the theater. Sir Herbert listened to the thunder, then said that it would not do. On being informed that the thunder was real, he said, "That may satisfy the people outside, but we must do better." By the way, the term "steal one's thunder" comes from John Dennis (1657-1734), who invented a new way of producing thunder for the stage, but who was incensed when other theatrical managers stole his new method of producing thunder.[223]

• In his old age, Sir Ralph Richardson began to lose his memory—a major problem for an actor. He was determined to learn a particular script by David Storey, so he kept telephoning Mr. Storey to report his progress on learning the script—"I've got to page 17" ... "I've got to page 23" ... "I've got to page 27." Once, he called Mr. Storey to report, "I'm on page 17." Mr. Storey, surprised, said, "But you were on page 27 last week." Sir Ralph, also surprised, asked if he was sure, then said, "Oh, God, I'm going backwards. It's hopeless." Eventually, he learned the script.[224]

• Diana Rigg once was present at a performance of Shakespeare's *Two Gentlemen of Verona* in Stratford when the stagehands operating the revolving stage were intoxicated. They accelerated the revolving stage to such a speed that anyone who tried to get on the stage was promptly thrown off. By the way, Ms. Rigg once performed as Lady Macbeth in a matinee given for schoolchildren. Apparently, they had all been studying *Macbeth*, because they joined in and recited the "I have given suck" speech along with her.[225]

• A reporter once asked Irish playwright Brendan Behan, "What is the message of your play?" Mr. Behan replied, "Message? What do you think I am … a bloody telegram boy?" And when someone asked him if he had read a particular book, he replied, "I need sympathy. I only went to school half time—when they were teaching the writing. I missed the reading."[226]

• Judi Dench once performed in a production of *Macbeth* that was played straight through without an intermission. Marie Kean, who was playing the First Witch, once noticed that some schoolboys were hiding out in the boys' restroom instead of watching the play, so she scared them back into the theater by marching into the restroom in full makeup and hissing at them, "Get back in there!"[227]

• Sir Henry Irving once sat through an amateur production of Shakespeare's *Twelfth Night*—a production that had no intermissions. Immediately following the play, he was asked his opinion of the production. He replied, "Capital! Capital! Where's the lavatory?"[228]

War

• Themistocles was the ancient Athenian leader who advocated the building of a navy that was responsible for winning the battle of Salamis in 480 B.C.E., thus preserving Greek independence. A man from the island of Seriphus insulted Themistocles by saying that Athens, not himself, was responsible for his fame. Themistocles replied, "Quite right. No one would have heard of me if I were from Seriphus. No one would have heard of you if you were from Athens."[229]

• General Israel Putnam once told his troops during the Revolutionary War that he wanted only willing soldiers: "If there are any of you who are dissatisfied and who want to return home, they can step six paces out in front of the line." General Putnam then added, "But I'll shoot the first man that does step out."[230]

Wit

• Here are some examples of wit: 1) Sports writers Joe Williams and Heywood Broun were watching the Max Baer-Primo Carnera fight, in which Mr. Baer knocked Mr. Carnera down several times, yet Mr. Carnera kept getting up. Mr. Williams said, "Gosh, but the big fellow certainly can take it." Mr. Broun replied, "Yes, but he doesn't seem to know what to do with it." 2) Douglas Jerrold disliked bores. While walking along the street one day, he met a bore who asked him, "Well, Jerrold, what's going on?" Mr. Jerrold replied, "I am," and he did. 3) Harry Hershfield once passed the gloomy building that housed the Union League Club in New York City. Because an important member had died, black crepe had been hung on the windows. Looking at the black crepe, Mr. Hershfield said, "It does liven up the old place, doesn't it?" 4) Judge Kelly of Chicago told a jury in the early 20th century: "My friends, money is not all. It is not money that will mend a broken heart or reassemble the fragments of a dream. Money cannot brighten the hearth nor repair the portals of a broken home. I refer, of course, to Confederate money."[231]

• During the Jim Crow days, Pierre Monteux and Sir Rudolf Bing were riding in the Georgia countryside when they stopped to have tea. However, a black woman told them, "We only served colored." Mr. Monteux replied, "But we are colored—we are pink." By the way, during the Jim Crow days, Sir Rudolf Bing took African-American diva Leontyne Price to dinner in an Atlanta hotel's restaurant. In his *5000 Nights at the Opera*, an autobiography, he writes, "As we walked in, there was a sudden hush, which I greatly enjoyed." Also by the way, Sir Rudolf did much to integrate the Metropolitan Opera, but at least once he denied a black child a job. The opera was *Rosenkavalier*, and Sir Rudolf decided against portraying a Viennese widow as having three children—two white and one black. And in *Aida* he was shocked to see that two Nubian slaves looked white. On being told that the two men were actually African-American, he replied, "I don't care what they are—they can wear dark makeup like everyone else."[232]

• The ancient Greeks and Roman were frequently witty: 1) Phocion was against war. When the politician Hyperides asked when he would advocate war, Phocion replied, "When I see our young men volunteering for military service, our millionaires contributing to the war effort, and our politicians keeping their hands off the public money." 2) Pyrrhus, king of Epirus, fought two battles against the Romans. He won both battles, but lost very many senior officers, causing him to say, "One more victory against the Romans and we're beaten." (This is where we get the term "Pyrrhic victory.") 3) An ambassador spoke for a long time before an assembly of Spartans, then asked what message he should report back to his people. The Spartans replied, "Tell them that we found it as hard to listen as you did to stop speaking." 4) The Roman emperor Claudius died after eating poisoned mushrooms. Afterward, he was deified. His successor, Nero, thereafter referred to mushrooms as "the food of the gods."[233]

• Movie mogul Samuel Goldwyn knew exactly what he wanted in a movie: "What we want is a movie that starts with an earthquake and works its way up to a climax." He also knew what he wanted for the audience of one of his movies: "I don't care if it doesn't make a nickel. I just want every man, woman, and child in America to see it." Another good man who could provide memorable quotations was W. C. Fields, who said, "Somebody left the cork out of my lunch" and "I must have a drink of breakfast." By the way, Alistair Cooke could also be witty. He once called Greta Garbo "every man's fantasy mistress. She gave you the impression that, if your imagination had to sin, it could at least congratulate itself on its impeccable taste."[234]

• Wilson Mizner once was manager of the Strand Hotel, where he allowed many homeless people to sleep. Things became so hectic that Mr. Mizner once posted these signs: NO OPIUM SMOKING IN THE ELEVATORS and CARRY OUT YOUR OWN DEAD. By the way, Mr. Mizner originated the phrase "Never give a sucker an even break." (In real life, he was an easy touch for anyone who needed a handout.) Mr. Mizner also once said, "I never worry about money unless a rich man comes anywhere near me. Then I can't sleep until I find a way to get in on the take."[235]

• Franklin Pierce Adams wrote a long-running column that frequently used contributions by other humorists. At the end of each year, Mr. Adams gave a gold watch to the person who had contributed the most items to his column. Other than that, there was no remuneration. Once, Mr. Adams was asked why he didn't give the gold watch to the contributor of the best item. Mr. Adams thought a moment, then said, "There is no such thing as the 'best' contribution. The fact that any contribution is accepted by me means that it is peerless."[236]

• John Gielgud opened as King Lear at the Old Vic the day before he read at the funeral service of Mrs. Patrick Campbell. As he was leaving the church, he overheard two people talking about his performance as King Lear. One person said, "It was an exciting occasion at the Old Vic last night," and the other person answered, "Yes—until the curtain went up." Mr. Gielgud remembers thinking that Mrs. Campbell would have relished the remark.[237]

Work

• In most productions of *Swan Lake*, Odette commits suicide in the final act by jumping into a lake and drowning herself. At a 1981 rehearsal of the Sadler's Wells Royal Ballet, ballerina Galina Samsova went up to the place where her character was to jump to her death, but being unwilling to die in real life, she cautiously climbed down the platform. As a result, the choreographer, Peter Wright, made sure that in the future there would be two catchers to make sure that Ms. Samsova's stage jump would not be dangerous. By the way, makeup appears in the strangest places. To prepare their costumes for *Swan Lake*, the swans of Sadler's Wells Royal Ballet put the makeup called wet-white—the same makeup they apply to their faces and arms—to their pointe shoes to take the shine off.[238]

• Because of British Broadcasting Corporation regulations, Sir Adrian Boult was forced to retire as conductor from the BBC Symphony Orchestra in 1950 when he reached the age of 60. Sir Adrian resented his enforced retirement, which he regarded as being completely arbitrary. After his retirement, he accepted an invitation to serve as the orchestra's guest conductor for a performance. At the beginning of the rehearsal, he looked at the clock and saw that its hands had stuck together. He then said, "Get the clock going, or I'll stop the rehearsal in ten minutes' time—when the clock says so." BBC management took the threat seriously and removed the hands from the clock.[239]

• We associate George Frideric Handel's *Messiah* with Christmas, but during Handel's lifetime, it was always performed during the seasons of Lent and Easter. Normally, theaters were closed during Lent, but *Messiah* was considered religious enough to be performed at that time. By the way, Mr. Handel was a Lutheran, although early in his career he worked as an organist in a Calvinist church. The Calvinists may have been willing to hire Mr. Handel, despite his religion, because the previous organist, Johann Christoph Leporin, frequently showed up to work drunk.[240]

• Everyone believes that ballerinas lead a glamorous life, but it is hard work—and often low paying. Illaria Obidenna Ladré danced in the Diaghilev Ballet, where she was paid very little. She, like the other dancers, learned to brush her teeth when she was hungry but had no food to eat. By the way, Mr. Sergei Diaghilev, who was not supported by tax money, also suffered for his art. He had holes in his shoes and died with $6 in his pocket. (Many people are against the use of tax money to support the arts, but taxes are the price of civilization.)[241]

• A man once asked R' Pinchas of Koretz whether he would have a chance to enter the Garden of Eden, adding that in this life he had to work very hard but had nothing to show for it. R' Pinchas asked if the man set aside time each day for studying the Torah, but the man replied that he did not. R' Pinchas then said, "If in this world, where you labor and work so hard, you have nothing, then what do you expect to receive in the Garden of Eden, for which you are doing nothing?"[242]

• Constance Benson (1860-1946) worked with actor Stephen Phillips in 1886, when he was no longer interested in his career. While playing Prospero in Shakespeare's *Tempest* on stage, he pretended his wand was a fishing pole and dangled it over the orchestra pit. As the play proceeded, he murmured to Ms. Benson in asides which fish he had caught, and from which musical instrument he had caught them.[243]

• When dancers Ted Shawn and Ruth St. Denis were touring, the towns they performed in began to blend together after a while, and sometimes they forgot where they were. Once, they reached for their tour list to find out the name of the town they were in, but they didn't know the date, so the tour list was of no help. They ended up asking a policeman directing traffic, "Can you tell us the name of this town?"[244]

• Richard Strauss was once shocked to hear that a former pupil had asked for a year's leave from an orchestra in order to compose. According to Mr. Strauss, the pupil already had plenty of time to compose. Mr. Strauss reasoned that each day has 24 hours; therefore, once you take away eight hours for sleeping, and 12 hours for working, you still have four hours for composing.[245]

• African-American opera singer Betty Allen was born in Campbell, Ohio. Her talent for hard work came in part from her mother, who during the Depression earned $30 a week as a washerwoman—a lot of money for the time. Ms. Allen says, "She had two Maytags going all the time, from six o'clock in the morning 'til midnight."[246]

• Gioacchino Rossini wrote and produced his *opera buffa* masterpiece, *Il Barbiere di Siviglia*, very quickly. In fact, it was composed—and rehearsed and staged—in less than a month. When

Gaetano Donizetti, another fast worker, learned this, he said of Mr. Rossini, "Well, he always was lazy."[247]

• Near the end of his career, actor Ronald Colman did a bit part in the movie *Around the World in Eighty Days* and received in payment a Cadillac. When he was asked if he had really received a Cadillac as payment for one day's work, he replied, "No, for the work of a lifetime."[248]

• Italian soprano Claudia Muzio used to stay occasionally at the Grand Hotel in Milan, which displayed a portrait of Giuseppe Verdi in her apartment. One day, Ms. Muzio asked the portrait, "I wonder if you know how much work you have brought my way."[249]

Yom Kippur

• Long ago, on Yom Kippur, many faithful Jews waited for the Hasidic master Levi-Yitzhak of Berditchev to arrive to say prayers, but one hour passed, then another. Finally, Levi-Yitzhak showed up. When the faithful asked why he was so late, he explained that a man who was illiterate wanted to pray, but could not. Therefore, the man explained to God that he was illiterate and could do nothing more than decipher the letters of the alphabet—but God was wise and could create prayers more beautiful than he could. Therefore, the man gave God the letters of the alphabet and asked God to use them to write prayers. "That is why I am late," Levi-Yitzhak explained. "God was busy writing."[250]

Appendix A: Bibliography

Adler, Bill. *Jewish Wit and Wisdom*. New York: Dell Publishing Co., Inc, 1969.

Alda, Frances. *Men, Women, and Tenors*. Boston, MA: Houghton Mifflin Company, 1937.

Alley, Ken. *Awkward Christian Soldiers*. Wheaton, IL: Harold Shaw Publishers, 1998.

Ayre, Leslie. *The Wit of Music*. Boston, MA: Crescendo Publishing Company, 1969.

Barber, David W. *Bach, Beethoven, and the Boys*. Toronto, Canada: Sound and Vision, 1996.

Barber, David W. *Getting a Handel on Messiah*. Toronto, Canada: Sound and Vision, 1994.

Beecham, Thomas. A *Mingled Chime*. New York: Da Capo Press, 1976.

Benchley, Nathaniel. *Robert Benchley*. New York: McGraw-Hill Book Company, Inc., 1955.

Benson, Constance. *Mainly Players: Bensonian Memories*. London: Thornton Butterworth, Ltd., 1926.

Berry, Ralph, compiler and editor. *The Methuen Book of Shakespeare Anecdotes*. London: Methuen Drama, 1992.

Bing, Sir Rudolf. *5000 Nights at the Opera*. Garden City, NY: Doubleday and Company, Inc., 1972.

Borge, Victor, and Robert Sherman. *My Favorite Comedies in Music*. New York: Franklin Watts, 1980.

Borge, Victor, and Robert Sherman. *My Favorite Intermissions*. Garden City, NY: Doubleday and Co., Inc., 1971.

Boxer, Tim. *The Jewish Celebrity Hall of Fame*. New York: Shapolsky Publishers, 1987.

Boyden, John, collector. *Stick to the Music: Scores of Orchestral Tales*. London: Souvenir Press, 1992.

Bracken, Peg. *I Didn't Come Here to Argue*. New York: Harcourt, Brace and World, Inc., 1969.

Brandreth, Gyles. *Great Theatrical Disasters*. New York: St. Martin's Press, 1982.

Brown, Michèle and Ann O'Connor. *Hammer and Tongues: A Dictionary of Women's Wit and Humour*. London: J.M. Dent and Sons, Ltd., 1986.

Bryan III, J. *Merry Gentlemen (and One Lady)*. New York: Atheneum, 1985.

Burke, John. *Rogue's Progress: The Fabulous Adventures of Wilson Mizner*. New York: G.P. Putnam's Sons, 1975.

Caruso, Dorothy. *Enrico Caruso: His Life and Death*. New York: Simon and Schuster, Inc., 1945.

Chotzinoff, Samuel. *Toscanini: An Intimate Portrait*. New York: Alfred A. Knopf, 1956

Cott, Ted. *The Victor Book of Musical Fun*. New York: Simon and Schuster, Inc., 1945.

Crow, Bill. *Jazz Anecdotes*. New York: Oxford University Press, 1990.

Danilova, Alexandra. *Choura: The Memoirs of Alexandra Danilova*. New York: Alfred A. Knopf, 1986.

de Mille, Agnes. *Portrait Gallery*. Boston, MA: Houghton Mifflin Company, 1990.

Denver, Bob. *Gilligan, Maynard and Me*. New York: Carol Publishing Group, 1993.

Dolin, Anton. *Alicia Markova: Her Life and Art*. New York: Hermitage House, 1953.

Domingo, Plácido. *My First Forty Years*. New York: Alfred A Knopf, 1983.

Douglas, Nigel. *More Legendary Voices*. London: Andre Deutsch Limited, 1994.

Drucker, Hal, and Sid Lerner. *From the Desk Of*. Photographs by Sing-Si Schwartz. San Diego: Harcourt Brace Jovanovich, Publishers, 1989.

Ewen, David. *Dictators of the Baton*. Chicago, IL: Ziff-Davis Publishing Company, 1948.

Ewen, David. *Famous Conductors*. New York: Dodd, Mead & Company, 1966.

Farrell, Suzanne. *Holding On to the Air*. New York: Summit Books, 1990.

Ferguson, John, compiler and translator. *The Wit of the Greeks and Romans*. London: Leslie Frewin, 1968.

Finck, Henry T. *Musical Laughs*. New York: Funk & Wagnalls Company, 1924.

Fonteyn, Margot. *Autobiography*. New York: Alfred A. Knopf, 1976.

Ford, Carin T. *Legends of American Dance and Choreography*. Berkeley Heights, NJ: Enslow Publications, Inc., 2000.

Ford, Corey. *The Time of Laughter*. Boston, MA: Little, Brown and Company, 1967.

Fountain, Richard, compiler. *The Wit of the Wig*. London: Leslie Frewin Publishers, Limited, 1968.

Frank, Rusty E. *Tap! The Greatest Tap Dance Stars and Their Stories, 1900-1955*. New York: William Morrow and Company, Inc., 1990.

Franks, A.H., editor. *Pavlova: A Collection of Memoirs*. New York: Da Capo Press, Inc., 1956.

Furst, Herbert. *The New Anecdotes of Painters and Paintings*. London: The Bodley Head, Ltd., 1926.

Garden, Mary, and Louis Biancolli. *Mary Garden's Story*. New York: Simon and Schuster, Inc., 1951.

Gielgud, John. *Distinguished Company*. London: Heinemann, 1972.

Goodman, Jack, and Albert Rice. *I Wish I'd Said That!* New York: Simon and Schuster, 1935.

Greskovic, Robert. *Ballet 101*. New York: Hyperion, 1998.

Groover, David L., and Cecil C. Conner, Jr. *Skeletons from the Opera Closet*. New York: St. Martin's Press, 1986.

Gruen, John. *People Who Dance*. Pennington, NJ: Princeton Book Company, 1988.

Halliwell, Leslie. *The Filmgoer's Book of Quotes*. New Rochelle, NY: Arlington House Publishers, 1973.

Haskins, Jim, and N.R. Mitgang. *Mr. Bojangles: The Story of Bill Robinson*. New York: William Morrow and Company, Inc., 1988.

Hay, Peter. *Broadway Anecdotes*. New York: Oxford University Press, 1989.

Hecht, Ben. *Charlie: The Improbable Life and Times of Charles MacArthur*. New York: Harper & Brothers, Publishers, 1957.

Henry, Lewis C. *Humorous Anecdotes About Famous People*. Garden City, NY: Halcyon House, 1948.

Hewlett-Davies, Barry, editor and compiler. *A Night at the Opera*. New York: St. Martin's Press, 1980.

Heylbut, Rose, and Aimé Gerber. *Backstage at the Opera*. New York: Thomas Y. Crowell Company, 1937.

Himelstein, Shmuel. *A Touch of Wisdom, A Touch of Wit*. Brooklyn, NY: Mesorah Publications, Limited, 1991.

Himelstein, Shmuel. *Words of Wisdom, Words of Wit*. Brooklyn, NY: Mesorah Publications, Ltd., 1993.

Holloway, Stanley. *Wiv a Little Bit O' Luck*. As told to Dick Richards. New York: Stein and Day, Publishers, 1967.

Hope, Bob. With Bob Thomas. *The Road to Hollywood: My Forty-Year Love Affair With the Movies*. Garden City, NY: Doubleday & Company, Inc., 1977.

Huggett, Richard. *Supernatural on Stage: Ghosts and Superstitions of the Theatre*. New York: Taplinger Publishing Company, 1975.

Humphrey, Laning, compiler. *The Humor of Music and Other Oddities in the Art*. Boston, MA: Crescendo Publishing Company, 1971.

Hyams, Joe. *Zen in the Martial Arts*. New York: Bantam Books, 1979.

Irving, Gordon, compiler. *The Wit of the Scots*. London: Leslie Frewin Publishers, Inc., 1969.

Isenberg, Barbara. *State of the Arts: California Artists Talk About Their Work.* Chicago, IL: Ivan R. Dee, 2000.

Jackson, Kathy Merlock, editor. *Walt Disney Conversations.* Jackson, Mississippi: University Press of Mississippi, 2006.

Jerome, Jerome K. *On the Stage—and Off: The Brief Career of a Would-Be Actor.* Wolfeboro Falls, NH: Alan Sutton Publishing, Inc., 1991.

Jillette, Penn. *God, No! Signs You May Already be an Atheist and Other Magical Tales.* New York: Simon and Schuster, 2011.

Johnson, Russell, and Steve Cox. *Here on Gilligan's Isle.* New York: HarperCollins Publishers, Inc., 1993.

Kanner, Bernice. *The 100 Best TV Commercials ... and Why They Worked.* New York: Times Books, 1999.

Karkar, Jack and Waltraud, compilers and editors. *... And They Danced On.* Wausau, WI: Aardvark Enterprises, 1989.

Kaufmann, Helen L. *Anecdotes of Music and Musicians.* New York: Grosset & Dunlap, Publishers, 1960.

Kelly, Richard. *The Andy Griffith Show.* Winston-Salem, N.C.: John F. Blair, Publisher, 1981.

Klosty, James, editor and photographer. *Merce Cunningham.* New York: Saturday Review Press/E.P. Dutton and Co., Inc, 1975.

Kristy, Davida. *George Balanchine: American Ballet Master.* Minneapolis, MN: Lerner Publications Company, 1996.

Krohn, Katherine E. *Marilyn Monroe: Norma Jeane's Dream.* Minneapolis, MN: Lerner Publications Company, 1997.

Krull, Kathleen. *Lives of the Artists: Masterpieces, Messes (and What the Neighbors Thought).* San Diego, CA: Harcourt Brace & Company, 1995.

Krull, Kathleen. *Lives of the Writers: Comedies, Tragedies (And What the Neighbors Thought).* San Diego, California: Harcourt Brace & Company, 1994.

Ladré, Illaria Obidenna. *Illaria Obidenna Ladré: Memoirs of a Child of Theatre Street.* With Nancy Whyte. Seattle, WA: The Author, 1988.

Lahee, Henry C. *Famous Singers of To-day and Yesterday.* Boston: L.C. Page and Company, 1898.

Levant, Oscar. *A Smattering of Ignorance.* New York: Doubleday, Doran, and Co., 1940.

Linkletter, Art. *I Wish I'd Said That! My Favorite Ad-Libs of All Time.* Garden City, NY: Doubleday & Co., Inc., 1968.

Macnee, Patrick. *The Avengers and Me.* With Dave Rogers. New York: TV Books, 1997.

Makarova, Natalia. *A Dance Autobiography*. Edited by Gennady Smakov. New York: Alfred A Knopf, Inc., 1979.

Markova, Alicia. *Giselle and Me*. New York: The Vanguard Press, Inc., 1960.

Markova, Alicia. *Markova Remembers*. Boston, MA: Little, Brown and Company, 1986.

Mapleson, Colonel J.H. *The Mapleson Memoirs: The Career of an Operatic Impresario, 1858-1888*. Edited by Harold Rosenthal. New York: Appleton-Century, 1966.

Marinacci, Barbara. *Leading Ladies: A Gallery of Famous Actresses*. New York: Dodd, Mead and Company, 1961.

Marx, Samuel. *Broadway Portraits*. New York: Donald Flamm, Inc., 1929.

Massine, Léonide. *My Life in Ballet*. Edited by Phyllis Hartnoll and Robert Rubens. London: Macmillan and Co., Ltd., 1968.

Matz, Mary Jane. *Opera Stars in the Sun: Intimate Glimpses of Metropolitan Personalities*. New York: Farrar, Straus, and Cudahy, 1955.

May, Robin, compiler. *The Wit of the Theatre*. London: Leslie Frewin, 1969.

McCann, Sean, compiler. *The Wit of Brendan Behan*. London: Leslie Frewin Publishers, Ltd., 1968.

Meek, Harold. *Horn and Conductor: Reminiscences of a Practitioner with a Few Words of Advice*. Rochester, NY: University of Rochester Press, 1997.

Miller, John. *Judi Dench: With a Crack in Her Voice*. New York: Welcome Rain Publishers, 2000.

Miller, John. *Ralph Richardson: The Authorized Biography*. London: Sidgwick and Jackson, 1995.

Montague, Sarah. *Pas de Deux: Great Partnerships in Dance*. New York: Universe Books, 1981.

Mour, Stanley I. *American Jazz Musicians*. Springfield, NJ: Enslow Publications, Inc., 1998.

Neale, Wendy. *Ballet Life Behind the Scenes*. New York: Crown Publishers, Inc., 1982.

Newman, Barbara and Leslie E. Spatt. *Swan Lake*. London: Dance Books, 1983.

Peterson, T.F. *Nightwork: A History of Hacks and Pranks at MIT*. Cambridge, Massachusetts: MIT Press, 2011.

Old, Wendie C. *Duke Ellington: Giant of Jazz*. Springfield, NJ: Enslow Publications, Inc., 1996.

Orgill, Roxane. *Shout, Sister, Shout!* New York: Margaret K. McElderry Books, 2001.

Procter-Gregg, Humphrey. *Beecham Remembered*. London: Gerald Duckworth & Company Limited, 1976.

Rigg, Diana, compiler. *No Turn Unstoned: The Worst Ever Theatrical Reviews*. Los Angeles, CA: Silman-James Press, 1982.

Robinson, Simon. *A Year With Rudolf Nureyev*. With Derek Robinson. London: Robert Hale Limited, 1997.

Rossi, Alfred. *Astonish Us in the Morning: Tyrone Guthrie Remembered*. London: Hutchinson & Co., Publishers, 1977.

Russell, Anna. *I'm Not Making This Up, You Know: The Autobiography of the Queen of Musical Parody*. New York: The Continuum Publishing Company, 1985.

Savage, Richard Temple. *A Voice from the Pit*. Newton Abbot; North Pomfret, VT: David & Charles, 1988.

Shawn, Ted. *One Thousand and One Night Stands*. With Gray Poole. New York: Da Capo Press, Inc., 1979.

Slezak, Leo. *Song of Motley*. New York: Arno Press, 1977.

Story, Rosalyn M. *And So I Sing: African-American Divas of Opera and Concert*. New York: Warner Books, 1990.

Stryk, Lucien and Takashi Ikemoto, selectors and translators. *Zen: Poems, Prayers, Sermons, Anecdotes, Interviews*. Chicago, IL: Swallow Press, 1981.

Tallchief, Maria. *Maria Tallchief: America's Prima Ballerina*. With Larry Kaplan. New York: Henry Holt and Company, 1997.

Telushkin, Rabbi Joseph. *Jewish Humor: What the Best Jewish Jokes Say About the Jews*. New York: William Morrow and Company, 1992.

Telushkin, Rabbi Joseph. *Jewish Wisdom: Ethical, Spiritual, and Historical Lessons from the Great Works and Thinkers*. New York: William Morrow and Company, Inc., 1994.

Terry, Walter. *Ted Shawn: Father of American Dance*. New York: The Dial Press, 1976.

Wagenknecht, Edward. *Merely Players*. Norman, OK: University of Oklahoma Press, 1966.

Wagner, Alan. *Prima Donnas and Other Wild Beasts*. Larchmont, NY: Argonaut Books, 1961.

Wheatcroft, Andrew, compiler. *Dolin: Friends and Memories*. London and Henley: Routledge & Kegan Paul, 1982.

Wiesel, Elie. *Souls on Fire: Portraits and Legends of Hasidic Masters*. Translated from the French by Marion Wiesel. New York: Random House, 1972.

Woollcott, Alexander. *Enchanted Aisles*. New York: G.P. Putnam's Sons, 1924.

Woollcott, Alexander. *Shouts and Murmurs: Echoes of a Thousand and One Nights*. New York: The Century Co., 1922.

Appendix B: About the Author

It was a dark and stormy night. Suddenly a cry rang out, and on a hot summer night in 1954, Josephine, wife of Carl Bruce, gave birth to a boy — me. Unfortunately, this young married couple allowed Reuben Saturday, Josephine's brother, to name their first-born. Reuben, aka "The Joker," decided that Bruce was a nice name, so he decided to name me Bruce Bruce. I have gone by my middle name — David — ever since.

Being named Bruce David Bruce hasn't been all bad. Bank tellers remember me very quickly, so I don't often have to show an ID. It can be fun in charades, also. When I was a counselor as a teenager at Camp Echoing Hills in Warsaw, Ohio, a fellow counselor gave the signs for "sounds like" and "two words," then she pointed to a bruise on her leg twice. Bruise Bruise? Oh yeah, Bruce Bruce is the answer!

Uncle Reuben, by the way, gave me a haircut when I was in kindergarten. He cut my hair short and shaved a small bald spot on the back of my head. My mother wouldn't let me go to school until the bald spot grew out again.

Of all my brothers and sisters (six in all), I am the only transplant to Athens, Ohio. I was born in Newark, Ohio, and have lived all around Southeastern Ohio. However, I moved to Athens to go to Ohio University and have never left.

At Ohio U, I never could make up my mind whether to major in English or Philosophy, so I got a bachelor's degree with a double major in both areas, then I added a Master of Arts degree in English and a Master of Arts degree in Philosophy. Yes, I have my MAMA degree.

Currently, and for a long time to come (I eat fruits and veggies), I am spending my retirement writing books such as *Nadia Comaneci: Perfect 10*, *The Funniest People in Comedy*, *Homer's* Iliad: *A Retelling in Prose*, and *William Shakespeare's* Hamlet: *A Retelling in Prose*.

By the way, my sister Brenda Kennedy writes romances such as *A New Beginning* and *Shattered Dreams*.

Appendix C: Some Books by David Bruce

Anecdote Collections

250 Anecdotes About Opera
250 Anecdotes About Religion
250 Anecdotes About Religion: Volume 2
250 Music Anecdotes
Be a Work of Art: 250 Anecdotes and Stories
The Coolest People in Art: 250 Anecdotes
The Coolest People in the Arts: 250 Anecdotes
The Coolest People in Books: 250 Anecdotes
The Coolest People in Comedy: 250 Anecdotes
Create, Then Take a Break: 250 Anecdotes
Don't Fear the Reaper: 250 Anecdotes
The Funniest People in Art: 250 Anecdotes
The Funniest People in Books: 250 Anecdotes
The Funniest People in Books, Volume 2: 250 Anecdotes
The Funniest People in Books, Volume 3: 250 Anecdotes
The Funniest People in Comedy: 250 Anecdotes
The Funniest People in Dance: 250 Anecdotes
The Funniest People in Families: 250 Anecdotes
The Funniest People in Families, Volume 2: 250 Anecdotes
The Funniest People in Families, Volume 3: 250 Anecdotes
The Funniest People in Families, Volume 4: 250 Anecdotes
The Funniest People in Families, Volume 5: 250 Anecdotes
The Funniest People in Families, Volume 6: 250 Anecdotes
The Funniest People in Movies: 250 Anecdotes
The Funniest People in Music: 250 Anecdotes
The Funniest People in Music, Volume 2: 250 Anecdotes
The Funniest People in Music, Volume 3: 250 Anecdotes
The Funniest People in Neighborhoods: 250 Anecdotes
The Funniest People in Relationships: 250 Anecdotes
The Funniest People in Sports: 250 Anecdotes
The Funniest People in Sports, Volume 2: 250 Anecdotes
The Funniest People in Television and Radio: 250 Anecdotes
The Funniest People in Theater: 250 Anecdotes

The Funniest People Who Live Life: 250 Anecdotes
The Funniest People Who Live Life, Volume 2: 250 Anecdotes
The Kindest People Who Do Good Deeds, Volume 1: 250 Anecdotes
The Kindest People Who Do Good Deeds, Volume 2: 250 Anecdotes
Maximum Cool: 250 Anecdotes
The Most Interesting People in Movies: 250 Anecdotes
The Most Interesting People in Politics and History: 250 Anecdotes
The Most Interesting People in Politics and History, Volume 2: 250 Anecdotes
The Most Interesting People in Politics and History, Volume 3: 250 Anecdotes
The Most Interesting People in Religion: 250 Anecdotes
The Most Interesting People in Sports: 250 Anecdotes
The Most Interesting People Who Live Life: 250 Anecdotes
The Most Interesting People Who Live Life, Volume 2: 250 Anecdotes
Reality is Fabulous: 250 Anecdotes and Stories
Resist Psychic Death: 250 Anecdotes
Seize the Day: 250 Anecdotes and Stories

[1]Source: Stanley Holloway, *Wiv a Little Bit O' Luck*, pp. 72-73.

[2]Source: Katherine E. Krohn, *Marilyn Monroe: Norma Jeane's Dream*, pp. 69-71, 86.

[3]Source: Ralph Berry, compiler and editor, *The Methuen Book of Shakespeare Anecdotes*, p. 130.

[4]Source: Edward Wagenknecht, *Merely Players*, pp. 40, 43.

[5]Source: Michèle Brown and Ann O'Connor, *Hammer and Tongues*, p. 165.

[6]Source: Tim Boxer, *The Jewish Celebrity Hall of Fame*, p. 38.

[7]Source: Bob Denver, *Gilligan, Maynard and Me*, p. 91.

[8]Source: Michèle Brown and Ann O'Connor, *Hammer and Tongues*, p. 104.

[9]Source: Richard Huggett, *Supernatural on Stage*, p. 210.

[10]Source: Robin May, compiler, *The Wit of the Theatre*, pp. 118-119.

[11]Source: Russell Johnson and Steve Cox, *Here on Gilligan's Isle*, p. 173.

[12]Source: Anna Russell, *I'm Not Making This Up, You Know*, pp. 170-171, 183.

[13] Source: Kathleen Krull, *Lives of the Writers: Comedies, Tragedies (And What the Neighbors Thought)*, p. 23.

[14]Source: Leo Slezak, *Song of Motley*, p. 280.

[15]Source: Patrick Macnee, *The Avengers and Me*, p. 80.

[16]Source: Samuel Chotzinoff, *Toscanini: An Intimate Portrait*, pp. 72, 80.

[17]Source: Samuel Marx, *Broadway Portraits*, p. 30.

[18]Source: Gyles Brandreth, *Great Theatrical Disasters*, p. 76.

[19] Source: Silas Allen, "Stillwater resident rescues artwork from trash bin." NewsOK (Oklahoma). 25 August 2012 <http://newsok.com/stillwater-resident-rescues-artwork-from-trash-bin/article/3703986/?page=1>.

[20]Source: Kathleen Krull, *Lives of the Artists*, pp. 31, 45.

[21]Source: Herbert Furst, *The New Anecdotes of Painters and Paintings*, p. 54.

[22]Source: Kathleen Krull, *Lives of the Artists*, p. 23.

[23]Source: James Klosty, editor and photographer, *Merce Cunningham*, pp. 29, 51, 58.

[24]Source: Bernice Kanner, *The 100 Best TV Commercials*, pp. 65-66.

[25]Source: Alexander Woollcott, *Shouts and Murmurs*, pp. 194-195.

[26]Source: Nathaniel Benchley, *Robert Benchley*, pp. 186, 192-193.

[27]Source: Sarah Montague, *Pas de Deux*, p. 67.

[28]Source: Peg Bracken, *I Didn't Come Here to Argue*, pp. 47, 154.

[29]Source: Alexander Woollcott, *Enchanted Aisles*, p. 63.

[30] Source: M. Thomas Inge, editor, *Charles M. Schulz Conversations*, pp. 57-58.

[31]Source: Anton Dolin, *Alicia Markova: Her Life and Art*, pp. 114-115.

[32]Source: Barry Hewlett-Davies, *A Night at the Opera*, p. 14.

[33] Source: Barbara Isenberg, *State of the Arts: California Artists Talk About Their Work*, pp. 279-280.

[34] Source: Ana Samways, "30 Sep: Raunchy Poultry." Sideswipe. *New Zealand Herald.* <http://www.nzherald.co.nz/sideswipe-with-ana-samways/news/article.cfm?c_id=1503050&objectid=10837516>.

[35]Source: Ken Alley, *Awkward Christian Soldiers*, pp. 45, 48-49.

[36]Source: Wendie C. Old, *Duke Ellington: Giant of Jazz*, pp. 48, 74.

[37]Source: Andrew Wheatcroft, compiler, *Dolin: Friends and Memories*, pages are unnumbered.

[38]Source: Alice Patelson, *Portrait of a Dancer, Memories of Balanchine*, pp. 50, 86-87.

[39]Source: Simon Robinson, *A Year With Rudolf Nureyev*, p. 132.

[40] Source: Erin Grace, "Omaha schoolgirl dresses as a different historical figure each day." *Omaha World Herald* (Nebraska). 17 October 2012 <http://www.omaha.com/article/20121016/NEWS/710169942/1707#>.

[41]Source: Walter Terry, *Star Performance*, pp. 26, 30-31, 37, 39, 40.

[42]Source: Robert Greskovic, *Ballet 101*, pp. 20, 155-156.

[43]Source: Constance Benson, *Mainly Players*, pp. 130-131.

[44]Source: Alicia Markova, *Markova Remembers*, "Acknowledgements" and pp. 8, 10-11.

[45]Source: A.H. Franks, editor, *Pavlova: A Collection of Memoirs*, pp. 26-27, 48.

[46]Source: Richard Huggett, *Supernatural on Stage*, p. 41.

[47]Source: Samuel Marx, *Broadway Portraits*, p. 46, 58-59.

[48]Source: Corey Ford, *The Time of Laughter*, pp. 23-24.

[49] Source: Tim Boxer, *The Jewish Celebrity Hall of Fame*, p. 66.

[50] Source: Alexander Woollcott, *Shouts and Murmurs*, pp. 240-241.

[51] Source: Stanley Holloway, *Wiv a Little Bit O' Luck*, p. 124.

[52] Source: M. Thomas Inge, editor, *Charles M. Schulz Conversations*, pp. 14, 82-83.

[53] Source: Oscar Levant, *A Smattering of Ignorance*, pp. 7, 25, 41, 46.

[54] Source: David Ewen, *Famous Conductors*, pp. 40, 43, 90-91.

[55] Source: Harold Meek, *Horn and Conductor*, pp. 25-26.

[56] Source: David Ewen, *Dictators of the Baton*, pp. 91-92.

[57] Source: Plácido Domingo, *My First Forty Years*, pp. 106-107.

[58] Source: Humphrey Procter-Gregg, *Beecham Remembered*, p. 81, 118.

[59] Source: Leslie Ayre, *The Wit of Music*, p. 64.

[60] Source: Samuel Chotzinoff, *Toscanini: An Intimate Portrait*, p. 11.

[61] Source: David Ewen, *Famous Conductors*, p. 96.

[62] Source: Mary Garden and Louis Biancolli, *Mary Garden's Story*, p. 173.

[63] Source: Lynn Monty, "Paying It Forward." *Burlington Free Press* (Vermont). 8 August 2012 <http://blogs.burlingtonfreepress.com/btv/2012/08/08/paying-it-forward/>.

[64] Source: Lucien Stryk and Takashi Ikemoto, selectors and translators, *Zen: Poems, Prayers, Sermons, Anecdotes, Interviews*, p. xxxiii.

[65] Source: Lewis C. Henry, *Humorous Anecdotes About Famous People*, pp. 40, 53-54, 56.

[66] Source: Herbert Furst, *The New Anecdotes of Painters and Paintings*, pp. 9-10, 53.

[67] Source: Richard Fountain, compiler, *The Wit of the Wig*, p. 21.

[68] Source: Kathleen Krull, *Lives of the Writers: Comedies, Tragedies (And What the Neighbors Thought)*, pp. 35, 65.

[69] Source: Diana Rigg, compiler, *No Turn Unstoned*, pp. 72-73, 179.

[70] Source: Laning Humphrey, compiler, *The Humor of Music and Other Oddities in the Art*, p. 71.

[71] Source: Jeremy Nichols, "Introduction" of Jerome K. Jerome's *On the Stage—and Off*, p. xii.

[72] Source: James Klosty, editor and photographer, *Merce Cunningham*, pp. 21, 24, 52.

[73] Source: Rusty E. Frank, *Tap!*, p. 160.

[74] Source: Carin T. Ford, *Legends of American Dance and Choreography*, pp. 36, 38, 40.

[75] Source: Suzanne Farrell, *Holding On to the Air*, pp. 106-107.

[76] Source: Agnes de Mille, *Portrait Gallery*, pp. 27, 35.

[77] Source: Alexandra Danilova, *Choura*, p. 103.

[78] Source: Davida Kristy, *George Balanchine: American Ballet Master*, pp. 20, 90, 115.

[79] Source: Robert Greskovic, *Ballet 101*, pp. 70-71.

[80] Source: Sarah Montague, *Pas de Deux*, pp. 53, 56.

[81] Source: Wendy Neale, *Ballet Life Behind the Scenes*, p. 5.

[82] Source: Walter Terry, *Ted Shawn: Father of American Dance*, p. 31.

[83] Source: Alicia Markova, *Giselle and Me*, p. 88.

[84] Source: Walter Terry, *Star Performance*, pp. 135-136.

[85] Source: John Gielgud, *Distinguished Company*, p. 50.

[86] Source: Alfred Rossi, *Astonish Us in the Morning*, pp. 225, 294.

[87] Source: Jim Haskins and N.R. Mitgang, *Mr. Bojangles*, pp. 239-240, 282.

[88] Source: John Boyden, collector, *Stick to the Music: Scores of Orchestral Tales*, pp. 90-92.

[89] Source: Andrew Wheatcroft, compiler, *Dolin: Friends and Memories*, pages are unnumbered.

[90] Source: Anton Dolin, *Alicia Markova: Her Life and Art*, pp. 40, 44-45.

[91] Source: T.F. Peterson, *Nightwork: A History of Hacks and Pranks at MIT*, pp. 154-157.

[92] Source: Seth Roberts, "Tyler Cowen's Unusual Final Exam." Seth's Blog. 9 August 2012 <http://blog.sethroberts.net/2012/08/09/tyler-cowens-unusual-final-exam/>.

[93] Source: Natalia Makarova, *A Dance Autobiography*, p. 52.

[94] Source: Lucien Stryk and Takashi Ikemoto, selectors and translators, *Zen: Poems, Prayers, Sermons, Anecdotes, Interviews*, pp. 121, 146.

[95]Source: Harold Meek, *Horn and Conductor*, pp. 22, 26.

[96]Source: Joe Hyams, *Zen in the Martial Arts*,

[97] Source: Ana Samways, "June 4: Quick courier delivery." Sideswipe. *New Zealand Herald*. 4 June 2012 <http://www.nzherald.co.nz/ana-samways/news/article.cfm?a_id=53&objectid=10810507>.

[98]Source: John Gruen, *People Who Dance*, pp. 81, 151.

[99]Source: Agnes de Mille, *Portrait Gallery*, p. 139.

[100]Source: Ben Hecht, *Charlie: The Improbable Life and Times of Charles MacArthur*, p. 29.

[101]Source: Frances Alda, *Men, Women, and Tenors*, pp. 47.

[102]Source: Russell Johnson and Steve Cox, *Here on Gilligan's Isle*, pp. 175, 178.

[103]Source: Alexandra Danilova, *Choura*, pp. 84, 152.

[104]Source: Barbara Marinacci, *Leading Ladies: A Gallery of Famous Actresses*, pp. 276-277.

[105] Source: Lauren Davis, "Father draws his daughter silly superhero cartoons to convince her to eat her lunch." Io9. 9 September 2012 <http://io9.com/5941658/father-draws-his-daughter-silly-superhero-cartoons-to-convince-her-to-eat-her-lunch>.

[106] Source: Illaria Obidenna Ladré, *Illaria Obidenna Ladré: Memoirs of a Child of Theatre Street*, pp. 3-4.

[107]Source: Bill Adler, *Jewish Wit and Wisdom*, p. 86.

[108]Source: Suzanne Farrell, *Holding On to the Air*, p. 67.

[109]Source: Margot Fonteyn, *Autobiography*, pp. 23, 50.

[110] Source: Bill Crow, *Jazz Anecdotes*, pp. 8-9.

[111]Source: Mary Garden and Louis Biancolli, *Mary Garden's Story*, p. 225.

[112]Source: Sir Rudolf Bing, *5000 Nights at the Opera*, pp. 74, 86.

[113]Source: Mary Jane Matz, *Opera Stars in the Sun: Intimate Glimpses of Metropolitan Personalities*, pp. 38-39, 310.

[114]Source: Rose Heylbut and Aimé Gerber, *Backstage at the Opera*, pp. 136, 210.

[115]Source: Ted Cott, *The Victor Book of Musical Fun*, pp. 33, 52.

[116]Source: Leslie Ayre, *The Wit of Music*, p. 31.

[117]Source: Hal Drucker and Sid Lerner, *From the Desk Of*, p. 20.

[118]Source: Carin T. Ford, *Legends of American Dance and Choreography*, pp. 82-83.

[119]Source: Natalia Makarova, *A Dance Autobiography*, p. 117.

[120] Source: Penn Jillette, *God, No! Signs You May Already be an Atheist and Other Magical Tales*, p. 81.

[121]Source: Peg Bracken, *I Didn't Come Here to Argue*, pp. 113-114, 126.

[122]Source: J. Bryan III, *Merry Gentlemen (and One Lady)*, p. 49.

[123] Source: Tom Greenwood and Rod Beard, "Southfield Twp. voter appears to die, then asks 'Did I vote?'" *The Detroit News* (Michigan). 6 November 2012 <http://www.detroitnews.com/article/20121106/METRO02/211060410/ Southfield-Twp-voter-appears-die-then-asks-Did-vote- ?odyssey=tab%7Ctopnews%7Ctext%7CFRONTPAGE>.

[124]Source: A.H. Franks, editor, *Pavlova: A Collection of Memoirs*, pp. 28-29, 67-68.

[125] Source: Barbara Isenberg, *State of the Arts: California Artists Talk About Their Work*, p. 347.

[126]Source: Plácido Domingo, *My First Forty Years*, p. 218.

[127]Source: Anna Russell, *I'm Not Making This Up, You Know*, pp. 186-187.

[128]Source: Léonide Massine, *My Life in Ballet*, pp. 62, 45-46, 81.

[129]Source: Jack and Waltraud Karkar, compilers and editors, ... *And They Danced On*, p. 178.

[130]Source: Frances Alda, *Men, Women, and Tenors*, pp. 98, 129.

[131]Source: Thomas Beecham, *A Mingled Chime*, pp. 141, 154.

[132]Source: Margot Fonteyn, *Autobiography*, p. 258.

[133]Source: Richard Temple Savage, *A Voice from the Pit*, p. 50.

[134]Source: Sean McCann, compiler, *The Wit of Brendan Behan*, p. 82.

[135]Source: Walter Terry, *Ted Shawn: Father of American Dance*, p. 154.

[136]Source: Alexander Woollcott, *Enchanted Aisles*, pp. 140-141.

[137]Source: Alicia Markova, *Giselle and Me*, pp. 72, 74.

[138]Source: Barbara Marinacci, *Leading Ladies: A Gallery of Famous Actresses*, pp. 278-279.

[139]Source: Rose Heylbut and Aimé Gerber, *Backstage at the Opera*, pp. 187-188, 203-204.

[140]Source: Victor Borge and Robert Sherman, *My Favorite Intermissions*, pp. 108-109.

[141]Source: Jerome K. Jerome, *On the Stage—and Off*, pp. 65-66.

[142]Source: Jack and Waltraud Karkar, compilers and editors, ... *And They Danced On*, p. 188.

[143]Source: Wendie C. Old, *Duke Ellington: Giant of Jazz*, p. 80.

[144]Source: Roxane Orgill, *Shout, Sister, Shout!*, pp. 18, 23.

[145]Source: Wendy Neale, *Ballet Life Behind the Scenes*, pp. 88-89.

[146]Source: Gyles Brandreth, *Great Theatrical Disasters*, p. 78.

[147] Source: Alex, "FedEx: Founder Gambled His Last $5,000 at a Blackjack Table to Stave Off Bankruptcy." Neatorama. 10 October 2012 <http://www.neatorama.com/2012/10/10/FedEx-Founder-Gambled-His-Last-5000-at-a-Blackjack-Table-to-Stave-Off-Bankruptcy/>.

[148]Source: Shmuel Himelstein, *Words of Wisdom, Words of Wit*, p. 245.

[149]Source: Leo Slezak, *Song of Motley*, p. 274.

[150]Source: Colonel J. H. Mapleson, *The Mapleson Memoirs*, p. 158.

[151]Source: Bill Adler, *Jewish Wit and Wisdom*, pp. 33-34.

[152]Source: Léonide Massine, *My Life in Ballet*, pp. 47, 123.

[153]Source: Roxane Orgill, *Shout, Sister, Shout!*, pp. 64-66.

[154]Source: Shmuel Himelstein, *A Touch of Wisdom, A Touch of Wit*, p. 284.

[155]Source: Alfred Rossi, *Astonish Us in the Morning*, p. 282.

[156]Source: J. Bryan III, *Merry Gentlemen (and One Lady)*, pp. 205-206.

[157]Source: Henry C. Lahee, *Famous Singers of To-day and Yesterday*, pp. 100-101.

[158] Source: Bill Crow, *Jazz Anecdotes*, p. 36.

[159]Source: David W. Barber, *Bach, Beethoven, and the Boys*, pp. 15, 28, 47, 50, 57.

[160]Source: Richard Temple Savage, *A Voice from the Pit*, pp. 46-47, 53, 168-169.

[161]Source: Stanley I. Mour, *American Jazz Musicians*, pp. 21, 34, 69-70, 100.

[162]Source: Victor Borge and Robert Sherman, *My Favorite Comedies in Music*, pp. 129, 139.

[163]Source: Thomas Beecham, *A Mingled Chime*, pp. 63-64, 171-172.

[164]Source: Willie Nelson, *The Facts of Life and Other Dirty Jokes*, pp. 64, 162, 192.

[165]Source: David Ewen, *Dictators of the Baton*, pp. 28, 179.

[166]Source: Humphrey Procter-Gregg, *Beecham Remembered*, pp. 119-120.

[167]Source: Helen L. Kaufmann, *Anecdotes of Music and Musicians*, p. 25-27.

[168]Source: David W. Barber, *Getting a Handel on Messiah*, pp. 18, 74.

[169]Source: Henry T. Finck, *Musical Laughs*, pp. 96-97.

[170]Source: Victor Borge and Robert Sherman, *My Favorite Comedies in Music*, pp. 79, 91.

[171]Source: Oscar Levant, *A Smattering of Ignorance*, pp. 147, 267.

[172]Source: Victor Borge and Robert Sherman, *My Favorite Intermissions*, p. 67.

[173]Source: Art Linkletter, *I Wish I'd Said That!*, p. 116.

[174]Source: Ted Shawn, *One Thousand and One Night Stands*, p. 32.

[175]Source: Ben Hecht, *Charlie: The Improbable Life and Times of Charles MacArthur*, p. 19.

[176]Source: Laning Humphrey, compiler, *The Humor of Music and Other Oddities in the Art*, p. 75.

[177]Source: John Burke, *Rogue's Progress: The Fabulous Adventures of Wilson Mizner*, p. 215.

[178]Source: Willie Nelson, *The Facts of Life and Other Dirty Jokes*, pp. 51-52.

[179]Source: Dorothy Caruso, *Enrico Caruso: His Life and Death*, p. 38.

[180]Source: Colonel J. H. Mapleson, *The Mapleson Memoirs*, pp. 158-159.

[181]Source: Alan Wagner, *Prima Donnas and Other Wild Beasts*, pp. 122-124.

[182]Source: David L. Groover and Cecil C. Conner, Jr., *Skeletons from the Opera Closet*, p. 13.

[183]Source: Mary Jane Matz, *Opera Stars in the Sun: Intimate Glimpses of Metropolitan Personalities*, pp. 12, 61-62.

[184]Source: Rosalyn M. Story, *And So I Sing: African-American Divas of Opera and Concert*, pp. 118, 123.

[185]Source: Katherine E. Krohn, *Marilyn Monroe: Norma Jeane's Dream*, pp. 7-8, 12, 109-110.

[186] Source: Kathy Merlock Jackson, editor. *Walt Disney Conversations,*. 55.

[187] Source: Penn Jillette, *God, No! Signs You May Already be an Atheist and Other Magical Tales*, pp. 44-45.

[188]Source: Nigel Douglas, *More Legendary Voices*, pp. 100, 105, 175, 230.

[189] Source: T.F. Peterson, *Nightwork: A History of Hacks and Pranks at MIT*, pp. 128, 138-139.

[190]Source: Henry T. Finck, *Musical Laughs*, pp. 91-92.

[191]Source: Bob Denver, *Gilligan, Maynard and Me*, p. 145.

[192]Source: John Miller, *Judi Dench: With a Crack in Her Voice*, p. 80.

[193]Source: Art Linkletter, *I Wish I'd Said That!*, p. 68.

[194]Source: Peter Hay, *Broadway Anecdotes*, pp. 296-297.

[195]Source: Elie Wiesel, *Souls on Fire*, p. 70.

[196]Source: Rusty E. Frank, *Tap!*, p. 40.

[197] Source: "The 25 Most Powerful TV Shows of the Last 25 Years." *Mental Floss.* 12 October 2012 <http://www.mentalfloss.com/blogs/archives/146530#ixzz29Gxwx3gR>.

[198]Source: Rabbi Joseph Telushkin, *Jewish Wisdom*, p. 132.

[199]Source: Edward Wagenknecht, *Merely Players*, pp. 71, 73.

[200]Source: John Miller, *Ralph Richardson*, pp. 135-136.

[201]Source: Jim Haskins and N.R. Mitgang, *Mr. Bojangles*, pp. 241-242.

[202]Source: Alan Wagner, *Prima Donnas and Other Wild Beasts*, pp. 64-65.

[203] Source: Kathy Merlock Jackson, editor. *Walt Disney Conversations*, pp. 57, 125.

[204]Source: Richard Kelly, *The Andy Griffith Show*, pp. 115, 118.

[205]Source: Bob Hope, *The Road to Hollywood*, p. 75.

[206]Source: Alicia Markova, *Markova Remembers*, p. 78.

[207]Source: John Burke, *Rogue's Progress: The Fabulous Adventures of Wilson Mizner*, p. 177.

[208]Source: Nathaniel Benchley, *Robert Benchley*, p. 170.

[209] Source: Maria Tallchief, *Maria Tallchief: America's Prima Ballerina*, pp. 55, 90.

[210]Source: Gordon Irving, compiler, *The Wit of the Scots*, p. 69.

[211]Source: Barry Hewlett-Davies, *A Night at the Opera*, p. 65.

[212]Source: Richard Fountain, compiler, *The Wit of the Wig*, p. 56.

[213]Source: Rabbi Joseph Telushkin, *Jewish Wisdom*, pp. 58-59.

[214]Source: Rabbi Joseph Telushkin, *Jewish Humor*, pp. 171-172.

[215]Source: Rabbi Joseph Telushkin, *Jewish Humor*, p. 223.

[216]Source: Gordon Irving, compiler, *The Wit of the Scots*, pp. 32, 52, 56.

[217]Source: Ken Alley, *Awkward Christian Soldiers*, pp. 28, 92-93.

[218]Source: Shmuel Himelstein, *Words of Wisdom, Words of Wit*, p. 66.

[219] Source: "The 25 Most Powerful TV Shows of the Last 25 Years." *Mental Floss*. 12 October 2012 <http://www.mentalfloss.com/blogs/archives/146530#ixzz29Gxwx3gR>.

[220]Source: Patrick Macnee, *The Avengers and Me*, p. 100.

[221]Source: Richard Kelly, *The Andy Griffith Show*, pp. 42, 113.

[222] Source: Bernice Kanner, *The 100 Best TV Commercials*, p. 182.

[223]Source: Ralph Berry, compiler and editor, *The Methuen Book of Shakespeare Anecdotes*, pp. 17, 114.

[224]Source: John Miller, *Ralph Richardson*, pp. 308-309.

[225]Source: Diana Rigg, compiler, *No Turn Unstoned*, pp. 164, 181.

[226]Source: Sean McCann, compiler, *The Wit of Brendan Behan*, pp. 25, 135.

[227] Source: John Miller, *Judi Dench: With a Crack in Her Voice*, p. 146.

[228]Source: Robin May, compiler, *The Wit of the Theatre*, p. 43.

[229]Source: John Ferguson, compiler and translator, *The Wit of the Greeks and Romans*, p. 84.

[230]Source: Lewis C. Henry, *Humorous Anecdotes About Famous People*, p. 16.

[231]Source: Jack Goodman and Albert Rice, *I Wish I'd Said That!* , pp. 69-70, 82-83, 121.

[232]Source: Sir Rudolf Bing, *5000 Nights at the Opera*, pp. 253-254.

[233]Source: John Ferguson, compiler and translator, *The Wit of the Greeks and Romans*, pp. 15, 22, 73, 88.

[234]Source: Leslie Halliwell, *The Filmgoer's Book of Quotes*, pp. 68, 83, 86.

[235]Source: Peter Hay, *Broadway Anecdotes*, p. 65.

[236]Source: Corey Ford, *The Time of Laughter*, pp. 14-15.

[237]Source: John Gielgud, *Distinguished Company*, p. 39.

[238]Source: Barbara Newman and Leslie E. Spatt, *Swan Lake*, pp. 15, 104, 106.

[239]Source: John Boyden, collector, *Stick to the Music: Scores of Orchestral Tales*, p. 29.

[240]Source: David W. Barber, *Getting a Handel on Messiah*, pp. 21, 84-85.

[241]Source: Illaria Obidenna Ladré, *Illaria Obidenna Ladré: Memoirs of a Child of Theatre Street*, pp. 16, 20.

[242]Source: Shmuel Himelstein, *A Touch of Wisdom, A Touch of Wit*, pp. 60-61.

[243]Source: Constance Benson, *Mainly Players*, p. 66.

[244]Source: Ted Shawn, *One Thousand and One Night Stands*, p. 152.

[245]Source: Helen L. Kaufmann, *Anecdotes of Music and Musicians*, p. 204.

[246]Source: Rosalyn M. Story, *And So I Sing: African-American Divas of Opera and Concert*, p. 134.

[247]Source: David L. Groover and Cecil C. Conner, Jr., *Skeletons from the Opera Closet*, p. 31.

[248]Source: Leslie Halliwell, *The Filmgoer's Book of Quotes*, pp. 171-172.

[249]Source: Nigel Douglas, *More Legendary Voices*, p. 205.

[250]Source: Elie Wiesel, *Souls on Fire*, p. 109.

www.ingramcontent.com/pod-product-compliance
Lightning Source LLC
Chambersburg PA
CBHW051234160726
47994CB00002B/871